CHRIST IN THE LITURGY

Christ in the Liturgy

BY

Dom Illtyd Trethowan
Monk of Downside Abbey

SHEED AND WARD
LONDON AND NEW YORK

ORDER OF THE HOLY CROSS
WEST PARK, NEW YORK

FIRST PUBLISHED 1952
BY SHEED AND WARD, LTD.
110/111 FLEET STREET
LONDON, E.C.4
AND
SHEED AND WARD INC.
840 BROADWAY
NEW YORK, 3

IMPRIMATUR : E. MORROGH BERNARD
VIC. GEN.
WESTMONASTERII, DIE 20a
SEPTEMBRIS 1951
PERMISSU SUPERIORUM O.S.B.

PRINTED AND MADE IN GREAT BRITAIN BY
FLETCHER AND SON LTD, NORWICH AND
THE LEIGHTON-STRAKER BOOKBINDING CO. LTD, LONDON

To

Dr Hedwig von Skoda

CONTENTS

CONTENTS

PREFACE

IN THE SPRING OF 1950 I WAS INVITED TO GIVE A COURSE OF twelve lectures on the Liturgy at a Catholic International Meeting held at Friedenweiler in the Black Forest during the last fortnight of the following September. The general subject of the Meeting was "Christ the Centre of the World", and these lectures were designed to fit in with it. They are published as the chapters of this book, substantially in the form in which they were delivered, with the exception of the fourth, a somewhat technical discussion of the eucharistic symbolism, which has been published in *The Downside Review* (Autumn, 1950); its main conclusions have been embodied in the third chapter, which has been to some extent recast in the process. The lecture which appears here as the Epilogue had been delivered at the Newman International Centre in London the previous year; since it brought out a point of view which underlay the whole exposition, it seemed legitimate and useful to reproduce it. The circumstances of the Friedenweiler Meeting also account for the special insistence upon the laity's participation in the Liturgy. And it seemed only right to offer the dedication to the lady whose devotion to Catholic truth and to the cause of international relations was the origin and the directing force of that meeting.

I should like to make it clear at the outset that the greater part of this book is *œuvre de vulgarisation*: it aims at summarizing for the convenience of the English reader the work of contemporary theologians and liturgists and is largely derived from French sources; it is inevitably "scrappy" and intended only as a stimulus. The Catholic who wishes to extend his knowledge and understanding of the Liturgy beyond the point to which the notes in his Missal will lead him finds himself faced with a certain difficulty. A set of volumes on the Liturgical Year, for example, is at once too much and too little for his immediate purposes. He is not yet prepared to cope with a mass of detail, and he feels the need for a compendious treatment of the subject, showing its main outlines, integrating it into a general

outlook upon life and relating it to the particular conditions of
his time. A glance at the chapter-headings will indicate at once
how I have tried to meet the need in some small measure. It has
been a great satisfaction to find in M. Louis Kammerer's
article on missals for the laity in *La Maison Dieu* 23, which has
just appeared (Nov. 1950), an agreement about this need and a
series of recommendations to writers of books like the present
which I may claim to have adopted in advance.

In some of these chapters I am drawing on work already
published in periodicals, and I have to thank Burns Oates and
Washbourne Ltd., and the Editors of *The Clergy Review*,
Liturgy and *The Lock Bulletin* for permitting me to do so. The
second and third chapters also incorporate a number of paragraphs from my essay "The Catholic Action" published in
Essays in Reconstruction (Sheed and Ward, 1946), and they are
based to some extent on articles published in *The Downside
Review* in recent years. But the ground has been worked over
afresh, and the treatment is, I hope, simpler and at the same
time less superficial than in my previous essays on the Mass.
Those were written in more or less close connexion with the
publication of *The Christian Sacrifice*, my translation of Canon
Masure's *Le Sacrifice du Chef*, and dealt largely with matters of
current controversy. Here I have attempted a "straight" account
of what seems to me to be true.

This may be considered a sort of supplement to *Certainty*
(Dacre Press, 1948) in so far as it develops from time to time
some of the conclusions reached in that book; an indulgent
critic pertinently remarked that signposts seemed to be erected in
Certainty without any precise indication of where they were
leading to, and I hope that a few glimpses of a somewhat un-
frequented country may be afforded in the course of these
chapters. (There does not seem any likelihood that I shall be
able to penetrate further into it in the visible future.) The
reader who feels that he is getting lost even on the short excur-
sions which I shall offer him will find that he can easily regain
the main road by turning a page or two.

For advice on particular points I am indebted to Fr Cuthbert
King, S.J., Fr Clifford Howell, S.J., Mr Lancelot C. Sheppard
and several Downside monks.

I

WHAT IS THE LITURGY?

THOSE WHO ARE PREPARED TO SPEND SOME TIME THINKING about liturgical worship are not likely to have the usual prejudices against it. Nevertheless it will be useful to begin by considering what they are. The most interesting one perhaps is that which sees in the Liturgy a form of escape from worship itself. Instead of facing up to the difficulties of prayer, so some people think, those whose worship is essentially liturgical are really inventing excuses for themselves, deceiving themselves into supposing that they have done their duty by performing a ritual in obedience to a set of rules. And although a Catholic could hardly share this prejudice in the bald form in which it has just been described, some Catholics may feel a certain degree of sympathy with it.

The first point I would make is that they may be quite right to do so in particular cases. It is possible to confuse means with ends even in regard to the Liturgy, to acquire a specialized interest in it as a technique and to have no serious appreciation of it in its inward reality. You can have an interest in rubrics which is really on all fours with having a taste for railway time-tables; you can be interested in vestments from the millinery point of view; you can be a plainchant expert (up to a point) without any real understanding of the proper function of plain-chant. You can be simply an archaeologist. And the danger of allowing the Liturgy to become a mere routine is a very real one.

But the answer to the objection has begun to emerge in the very attempt to do justice to it. It is the inward reality of the Liturgy which gives value to all the rest. The mere performance of a ritual is not what ought to be meant by "Liturgy". Yet it must be added at once that this does not make the externals unimportant. The inward reality in the Christian religion is to be found by means of externals. The Christian Sacraments are the means by which men are to be united with God. Even when they are ignorant of this truth, the principle holds—*extra ecclesiam nulla salus;* all grace comes from the *Incarnate* Word, living and working in his Mystical Body, the Catholic Church.

The necessity of liturgical worship follows from that. And the liturgical system is not just something which we have to use on particular occasions; it is the very texture of the Christian life. But it would take a long time to show the non-Christian that this is so, even if he were willing to accept the Christian fact as a hypothesis. If we consider some of his difficulties, it may help to strengthen our own grasp of the liturgical principle.

Our imaginary interlocutor might begin by saying that the Christian fact cannot do away with the necessity of worshipping in *spirit* the God whom it attests. All this liturgical paraphernalia seems to him against that. There may be visible means of grace; indeed, it seems both to fit in with the general scheme of human things and to follow from the character of the alleged Revelation. But the essential act of religion must surely lie in the direct intercourse of the individual with God, *solus cum Solo*. What are we to say about this?

First, I suppose, that our friend is only beginning to realize the implications of the Christian fact. He is accustomed to referring to the Church as a "body". But he has not yet appreciated the significance of this metaphor; a body is not merely a collection of functions all in dependence upon a single animating principle—the very fact that the functions are thus animated unites them not only with the principle but with one another, in such a way that it is positively misleading to describe them as forming a *collection* at all, unless we make it clear at the same time that the language is "provisional". That is to say, according to traditional Christian teaching, to talk about individuals simply in themselves makes only incomplete sense. You cannot define man satisfactorily without at the same time referring to God—without referring man to God. He is not only a rational animal but a praying one. You cannot, the Fathers said, refer the individual even to God *simply* as an individual. It is only as a member of the Mystical Body that he *really* makes sense. This has been brought out magnificently for our time by P. de Lubac in his *Catholicisme*, which has recently appeared in English.[1]

[1] P. de Lubac, *Catholicism*, trans. L. C. Sheppard, Burns Oates & Washbourne, 1950.

The whole purpose of mankind is to be united in the Incarnate Word, gathered up by Christ into a single unbroken whole. This is not the abolition but the fulfilment of the individual person. Until it occurs man has not properly achieved himself. That is his whole *meaning*.

Here we have a good illustration of the way in which the findings of reflective commonsense, otherwise called philosophy, are triumphantly verified by the Christian Revelation. It is impossible to work out a satisfactory ethical system which does not base itself on the principle of the common good on the one hand and on that of the "kingdom of ends", the inalienable value of the person, on the other. Unless we are to fall foul of one of these two principles, we must conclude that the individual person can achieve his full development only by devoting himself, according to his circumstances, to the common good. The Christian Revelation shows us the true character of the "kingdom of ends" and how to aim at it; and it tells us that it has begun already, in a germinal, developing form, on this earth. As I had occasion to write some years ago, "just as it is only by submission to reality that our mental development is possible, so it is by surrendering ourselves to God's plan for the world that we really find ourselves—by co-operating, keeping nothing back, in the work of the Redemption. ... This is the heart of the Liturgy."[1]

If we are each made for the vision of God, we must each will the accomplishment of his will—for all of us. Unless we are making God's will for the world our final criterion, we are not really seeking God. But these generalities are only the background of a reply to the objection with which we are concerned. It is all very well to claim that all true prayer links a man with his fellows as well as with God. The objector may allow that, and still say that he has not been answered. What he dislikes is this emphasis on participating in pre-arranged performances. Something of the kind is no doubt necessary; it is right that worship should be *expressed*, and publicly expressed. But the real business of prayer must go on at other times; it demands freedom of spirit, and solitude.

It may ease matters at this point to comment on the phrase

[1] *What is the Liturgy?* published by the Society of St Gregory, p. 4.

used above, "essentially liturgical" worship. It should not be taken to mean that there is no true worship outside the actual performance of the Church's Liturgy. What it means is that this performance is the centre and spring of our religion. To bring this out I may perhaps be allowed to quote myself again:

Is not the Saint's quasi-experimental knowledge of God in the silence of the heart greater, *more fruitful for the Church*, than his participation in the Church's psalmody? My answer is that the love of God is normally engendered by the Liturgy. It is the normal source of the spiritual life—and by normal I mean that it is the spiritual nourishment which the Church provides. By the Liturgy is meant the whole official prayer of the Church—pre-eminently the Mass, and, surrounding it, leading up to it, and so to speak continuing it, the canonical hours ... The more we can participate in it (that means in practice for most of us exclusively in the Mass) the more we are in the normal stream of Catholic holiness. God is not tied to sacramentals or to sacraments. But it is the ordinary disposition of his providence as revealed to us that we should become united more closely to him by the Liturgy. The silent prayer of the heart is the flowering of the soul fructified by the Liturgy. It is a preparation for a richer participation in the Liturgy. There may be exceptions, but I am speaking of norms. People have been known to say that they find the Liturgy distracting, that it hampers their prayers. At first one is inclined to think of the old story of the missionary priests who were saying office "privately" when martyrdom suddenly became a probability: "We had better stop"—one of them is supposed to have said—"and pray". But these people of whom I speak do not think that the Liturgy is not a prayer: but they do maintain that it can get in the way of what they might call pure prayer. I admit the difficulty. But I would suggest that it ought to be possible ideally to be as recollected during the Liturgy as at any other time. I would even suggest, rashly perhaps, that this is the very highest state of prayer. At any rate if people complain that they are distracted by the Mass we should all be content, I imagine, to leave their states of prayer out of our general scheme. Please do not think that I am gibing at mysticism. Contemplative prayer is surely in the normal development of the soul in grace. But its source is sacramental. A mystic who depreciated the sacraments would be suspect.[1]

Something remains to be said about freedom of spirit. All parties to the discussion are in favour of it, but it does not seem to mean the same thing to all of them. The masters of the spiritual life mean by freedom of spirit readiness to respond to the Holy Spirit's motions in the soul. Whatever you are doing, they say, unless you are engaged in some function for which your close attention is obviously indispensable, as in the case of the celebrant at Mass, follow God's leading, do not quench the Spirit, let yourself be drawn into his peace when he gives you the sign. It is worth noting that they seem to expect this to happen at least as much during the performance of the Liturgy as at other times. (Some people indeed are tempted to give up "mental prayer", because things never seem to "go well" except during the Liturgy. But that is another story.) When "freedom of spirit" is taken to mean anything different from this, we shall probably be wise to suspect it. It is likely to form part of a false anthropology, bound up with "striking out a line of one's own". Then it is desirable, I think, to point out that the Saints are the only people who are genuinely original. Bogus originality—flashiness and pose or sheer deceit—is easy. The Saints are real personalities, richly diversified. And they glory in having "one-track" minds, and in running counter to the silliness which is taken in by vague blanketing labels of that sort, whether vaguely pejorative like "one-track" or vaguely hortatory like "developing your personality" (a close relation to "freedom of spirit" taken in an untheological sense). We have come back to the theme of losing your soul to save it. The discipline of the Liturgy is the real road to freedom.

The Liturgy is an *instruction* in the precise sense of the word. When we put ourselves into the right attitude in his regard, God always instructs us, puts us to rights, and the Liturgy is the supreme example of this. When people are "put off" by the Liturgy, the chances are that they are not prepared to be put to

[1] *Ibid.* p. 5.

rights. In other words, so far from being opposed to contemplation, it is too contemplative for them. Contemplation means
letting God act upon you. "Adam sinned when he fell from
contemplation", said St Augustine in one of those casual
remarks of his which sum everything up. "Striking out a line of
one's own" is therefore the very last thing that is wanted. The
whole business of life is to discover what powers God is putting
into our hands and then to use them to the fullest possible
extent (the German word *Kunstleben* always suggests itself to
me in this connexion). Sometimes it is difficult to know what our
powers are, how our particular vocation is supposed to work
in these particular conjunctions; and then it may be our business
simply not to bother about being bothered. But the joy of the
Liturgy is that you know perfectly well what you are supposed
to be doing. Sometimes it may seem to be a rather pointless
sort of thing in itself—the Church's liturgical rules are not all
directly inspired by the Holy Spirit—but it is plainly what is
called for at the present moment. And if we approach the
Liturgy in this spirit, it is surprising how few things prove to be
pointless in themselves when we have begun to feel more or less
at home with the thing as a whole.

The original objection tends to recur at this point. You are
just running away from the real problems, we shall be told, and
finding satisfaction in playing a solemn game, obeying the rules
of your own invention. "A solemn game" is not a bad phrase for
the Liturgy. But "solemn" must be taken in its proper sense,
which has nothing to do with pomposity or hypocrisy but com-
bines the notes of festivity and dignity (Mr C. S. Lewis has said
some very good things about it in his *Preface to Paradise Lost*).
And "game" must be taken not in the sense of "make-believe"
but in that of relaxation, of letting oneself go. David dancing
before the ark is the accepted illustration of this. For the
Liturgy is fundamentally the *praise* of God, entering so far as
we can on this earth into his joy (Claudel's *le grand rire divin*).
We invent the rules only to the extent that we naturally express
our thanks to God "for his great glory" by using the visible
things of this world as they are meant to be used, our own
bodies included, making them the vehicles of the Spirit, saturat-
ing them with our intelligence. This is, I suppose, the final

function of art. When we say that the artist creates, what we should mean is that he "invents" his patterns in the etymological meaning of the word: he *finds* them. Just to say that art "holds up a mirror to nature" is to stop short before the really important thing about it: it does not merely illuminate for us the world of our direct experience—*natura naturata*—but the refractions of the Divine Mind—*Natura naturans*. Our liturgical performances are pre-arranged—in principle—by God. We achieve absolute spontaneity only when we find God, when we allow him to speak to us in the things that he has made, not exclusively in the secret of the heart, but everywhere—"if a man does not love his brother whom he sees ...". The great visions of the Old and New Testaments, the vision of the sixth chapter of Isaias and the vision of the Apocalypse, are in a liturgical setting.

At the beginning I said, "it is possible to be a plainchant expert (up to a point) without any real understanding of the proper function of plainchant". This was probably taken to mean—and it did mean—that you cannot have a real understanding of plainchant until you see that it is composed (the best of it, that is) by men who were expressing themselves musically *in prayer*. If you want to pray and you happen not to be more or less tone-deaf, then—in time, and given opportunity—you come to realize that it is saying what you want to say, musically, in the precise way in which it ought to be said. The man who is wholly absorbed in the technical side of it does not properly appreciate this. But it is now time to point out that he does see something. The original statement about him did after all make an affirmation as well as a denial; it gave him status as an expert. And even if we suppose him to know plainchant only from the outside, so to speak, he will be paying to God that unconscious implicit worship which is involved, I take it, in all artistic or aesthetic activity as such. We may be forced to suspect that some people remain on this level because they are unwilling to go beyond it—then music becomes a temptation for them. But in itself, properly used, not treated as an excuse, it is a stimulus. It seemed worth while bringing this out because sometimes well-intentioned people are inclined to regard the externals of the Liturgy with a certain suspicion on the ground that they are a spiritual luxury—useful, perhaps necessary up to a point, but not to be indulged in to excess. The point may perhaps be put in this way: that the values of the Liturgy do not cease to be aesthetic values when they are explicitly religious ones. "Oh! But he's simply enjoying himself", people may say. Not only is there nothing to be despised about enjoyment (on the contrary, God made us to be happy), but the artist's enjoyment is in itself a pure and spiritual thing. It is not to the point that his un-professional enjoyments may happen to be far less respectable.

For the well-intentioned people just mentioned another gloss on an earlier statement is called for at this stage. "It is possible", I observed, "to confuse means with ends even in regard to the Liturgy". There is no need to retract this remark, but it may easily have been taken as meaning more than it does. It does not mean that the Liturgy is simply a means to an end. The truth is that it is both a means and an end at the same time, because it is both casing, so to speak, and content. If people are allowed to say that it is *simply* a means to an end, they may go on to draw quite false conclusions. Union with God is the end, they will say, and the Liturgy is a means, indeed a very special sort of means, for gaining it, but not the only one. The claims of charity are supreme. And so on. It may even lead to the extreme view (if it can be called a view) according to which the Liturgy is merely a highly recommended preparation for the real busi-ness of life, whatever that may be supposed to be. And then there is no answer to those who say that you can have too much of a good thing, that we can't expect everyone to be liturgically minded ... but I spare you the rest.

The claims of charity are indeed supreme. But what do we want for our neighbours? That they should be united with God —we are all agreed about that. But this life which we want them to lead is the Church's life, that is, the Liturgy. It seems so very obvious, yet it is often misunderstood. There must be something wrong with our evangelizing efforts if, in their supposed inter-ests, that life which we intend to communicate becomes im-poverished, reduced to a shadow. It is often difficult, no doubt, to know how to apply our principles in this matter to particular circumstances. We may have to narrow the stream of our liturgical life at times, but only that it may flow more widely

later. There is also the familiar principle that prayer is the
highest form of the apostolate, and I mention it here because it
might seem to some as if in making that last concession I had
endangered it. Prayer is the highest form of the apostolate—but
that does not dispense us from spreading the Gospel; and this is
not to be done simply from the pulpit. Those of us who have
the opportunity to approach non-Catholics directly must not
suppose that we have done our whole duty by devoting all our
spare time to devout exercises, unless we are satisfied that we
have a special vocation in that respect. In the normal disposition
of God's providence, faith comes by hearing. It does not come
without prayer, on our part and on that of our non-Catholic
friends, but it does not normally come by prayer alone. Hence,
sometimes, an apparent clash between our duties, and then we
must rely on the Holy Spirit's guidance. But what is perfectly
clear is that if we allow social activities, educational projects or
whatever it may be, to deaden our appreciation of the liturgical
life, if we fail to keep it ever before our eyes as the goal and
raison d'être of our existences, then we have missed the wood for
the trees.

To sum up this matter then, ends and means may be confused
in two ways. We may turn the "means" element in the Liturgy
into an end, and that is the danger which gets on the whole a
better press and which therefore comes to mind more naturally.
But we may also turn the "end" element into a means, which is a
more insidious and often, in the long run, a more disastrous
confusion.

So far we have been dealing with objections of principle, and
as a result some sort of sketch of what the Liturgy is may have
emerged. But we have been considering it in ideal form, and
there is a whole range of objections based on the failure of the
existing Liturgy to conform to the ideal. Most of those had
better be left for more detailed treatment later, when the sketch
has been to some extent filled in. But it will be convenient to
glance at them at the outset. First we may take the objection that
the Liturgy as so far described seems to be the apanage of the
Christian who has already travelled far along the spiritual way
—this emphasis on joy, for example, is merely disheartening for
those who regard the whole business with some despondency and

even alarm. To bring things to a point, *are* the faithful rejoicing before the Lord when they come to Mass? It does not look much like it as a rule, in some parts of the world at any rate. They seem to be just sticking it out. What is the relevance, then, of all this talk about life and spontaneity? There may have been some truth in it at one time, but since then the Liturgy has fossilized, and the faithful, generally speaking, are now quite out of touch with it. The Roman Mass has not been altered in any but the slightest way for nearly 400 years. The Canonical Hours have become simply the priest's prayer book. No choirs sing them except monastic ones and a very few in cathedrals—only two or three choirs of cathedral canons sing them all (and mostly on one note, too). Even St Peter's in Rome has given it up. Plainchant is daunting enough, but Latin and the "cursing psalms" and bogus symbolism are even worse. It is all out of date.

That is a serious indictment, and although we are not yet in a position to assess it properly, it is only fair to say at once that it cannot be simply explained away. Some of the problems to which it draws attention are urgent. All that can be done at the moment is to suggest that they do not follow from the principles of the Liturgy itself and that there is no ground for turning our backs on these principles and working out a "more modern" spirituality. First, then, let us disclaim the notion that the Liturgy must always be actually enjoyed. It is leading us to joy, offering us joy, as I have said, but for a start it is hard work. It requires of us an asceticism which is even more searching than that which "more modern" forms of spirituality usually recommend to us. Nor is it in any way unreal or hypocritical to use liturgical prayers which are not expressing our immediate sentiments. A general desire to "grow into" the mind of the Liturgy is sufficient. And any sane psychologist knows that we bring about in ourselves the right dispositions by *doing* the sort of thing which corresponds with them.

This preliminary survey may be rounded off with some general considerations suggested by the supposed antinomy between the Liturgy and "modern spirituality". The lines of a solution have been indicated already, but it must be pointed out that there have been excesses in two directions. Not only has there been in recent centuries a failure to appreciate what the

Liturgy means, but there has been also in our own century an undiscriminating depreciation of modern devotional practices. We may wish that "unliturgical" devotions should give place, as an understanding of the Liturgy returns among us, to more traditional and more *solid* forms of worship. But it would be foolish to try to abolish them, at least until the ground is prepared. And it would be wrong to overlook the positive lessons which have been taught to us by "unliturgical" saints and spiritual writers. The great Spanish mystics of the 16th century are in a sense "unliturgical"; that is, they do not give prominence to the Liturgy, although they inevitably presuppose it. And we must attribute to their influence, however well-intentioned, a cutting down of liturgical observances. But it would be absurd to regard them as "individualists" who have no message for more enlightened people. They have given immortal testimony to the *end* which the whole system of liturgical observances is designed to promote, the closer union of the soul with God, to the reality of that life of grace which the Liturgy communicates to us, and to our need of developing that reality by opening to its influx the inmost recesses of our being. We may perhaps feel that this has led in practice to a good deal of morbid introspection. But it has certainly led to a great awakening. It has been a most emphatic protest against formalism and unreality in religion, against idle passivity, low ideals, the notion that our business on earth is simply to avoid mortal sin and make our Easter duties.

It is not, then, a question of choosing between the spirituality of the Liturgy and that of, say, Fr Baker, the author of *Holy Wisdom*, one of the most impressive statements in the English language of the primacy of contemplation—and the Liturgy is hardly mentioned in it. (For various reasons which do not concern us, Fr Baker's own participation in the Liturgy was reduced to a minimum, and this appears to be the explanation.) But it has been pointed out that we have only to bring our liturgical principles to our reading of Fr Baker to realize that so far from colliding with his teaching they reinforce and illumine it. Fr Baker's ascetical teaching is fundamentally that of the Liturgy. So is that of Père de Caussade. So is that of St Thérèse of Lisieux. There is the same insistence on our absolute dependence upon God, upon that fundamental *openness of mind* in his regard which is the source of all the virtues, upon that incorporation into Christ which is furthered, if we will allow it to be so, by each moment of our lives. In particular, Fr Baker emphasizes that prayer is itself the most thorough-going ascesis. The Liturgy drives this home. As we get to understand it better, it concentrates our minds upon the one thing necessary, pushes us gently but firmly below the surface of things to the heart of the matter, convinces us that life is not an affair of bits and pieces but a pattern which God is working out in us, which we must see as a whole, unified by a single purpose. The Liturgy is not an alternative to the "dark nights" of sense and spirit. Rather we are led through them in it by the surest road, that of the Church's prayer, Christ's prayer.

A single example must suffice to illustrate this supposed opposition between "types of spirituality". A "private" thanksgiving after Holy Communion is a relatively modern practice. "Liturgists" sometimes talk about it as if they disapproved of it.[1] They may not intend to produce this impression, but it is received. More than once I have come across enthusiastic accounts of the celebration of Mass in the first Christian centuries which emphasize the speed with which the proceedings are ended. Even the Post-Communion prayer is not really a thanksgiving, we are told; the faithful received Holy Communion and went off almost without a pause to take the Mass into the life of every day. All this is admirable, but for the suggestion that the modern custom is an undesirable one. It may be bound up in practice with the false idea that Holy Communion is a "private devotion". But, when we have shed this false idea, it seems rather unnecessary that we should feel constrained to discontinue our previous custom of remaining in the church for a few minutes at the end of Mass. If any "liturgist" really thinks this objectionable in itself, then he has something to learn from "modern spirituality": in fine, that the union of the individual soul with God, despite all that must be said about the Communion of Saints, does not cease to be that of an individual soul. But it is not to be supposed that he would think this, just as, if someone were to say "mental prayer is a modern

[1] Cf. the Encyclical *Mediator Dei*, 130 f.

invention", we should not suppose him to be denying the existence of the Desert Fathers, St Augustine, St Benedict and his innumerable sons.

The word "spirituality" has been occurring a good deal. It has a slightly unsatisfactory ring about it, a sort of tinniness; but such expressions can hardly be avoided. "The spiritual life" is another—so it may be well to end this chapter by emphasizing that the Liturgy has always the stamp of wholeness. We are not entering upon a special kind of life, but just *life*. The Church Catholic is the church to which all life belongs.

II

THE CHRISTIAN MYSTERY

MY PURPOSE THROUGHOUT IS TO SHOW IN SOME MEASURE how by participating in the Liturgy we are participating in the Christian Mystery. The obvious course, then, at this point, now that the preliminary objections have been considered, might seem to lie in an immediate examination of the most significant liturgical texts. But this is a method which would lead to insuperable difficulties. It is clear that the Liturgy expresses in an inimitable way all the truths which Catholics believe. It is possible to draw up a liturgical catechism, to articulate the Christian faith in the words of the Liturgy, as Dom Denis Rutledge has shown us.[1] This is in itself an admirable procedure. But, as he has found, it cannot be comprised within the limits of a single short volume, and it requires, even so, a considerable amount of introductory explanation. But could we not suppose that the introductory matter might be omitted here? I think not. The Liturgy pre-supposes an all-over grasp of theology which is not at all common nowadays. If we were to turn to the texts at once we should find that almost every one of them would lead us into lengthy developments; it would suggest lines of thought which would need to be pursued. We should move very slowly in our exami-nation of, say, the great Eucharistic Anaphora. It is perfectly true that the lack of an all-over grasp of theology, by which I mean not technicalities but a view of the Mystery itself as an indivisible whole, is itself due very largely to a lack of acquaint-ance with the Liturgy. But we have to remember that the liturgical rites have never been the sole source of a Christian's instruction. The word must be preached. Certainly the preach-ing of the word is part of the Liturgy. But many of us, for one reason or another, have not in fact received during the Liturgy the sort of instruction which prepares us for the liturgical texts. When we have received it the Liturgy will lead us further year

[1] In his *Catechism through the Liturgy*, London, Douglas Organ.

by year into the fuller meaning of it—and that is what I shall try
to show in the long run. But for the present we must be concerned with the Mystery itself. We shall go on to find that it is
present in the Liturgy. Only then can we see how it is also
shown forth by the words and gestures of the Liturgy, the sights
and sounds presented to us.

Our guide, to begin with, will be Dom Odo Casel, whose
book *Das Christliche Kultmysterium* appeared in a French
translation by Dom Hild, *Le Mystère du Culte*, in 1940. St Paul,
he reminds us, "sums up the whole of Christianity, the whole
gospel, in the word *mystery*. And it means for him *a divine
action*, the accomplishing of an eternal design on God's part
by an action which proceeds from God's eternity, which is
realized in time and in the world, and which finds its ultimate
achievement, its end, in the Eternal himself."[1] "This *mysterium*", he continues, "can be enunciated in the one word
Christ, referring both to the person of the Saviour and to his
Mystical Body which is the Church." This mystery was for long
hidden in the depths of the divinity, St Paul also tells us, but it
has now been revealed by the assumption of a human nature
into personal union with the Word. And because of man's sins
the mystery has become "an *economy*, a redemptive providence, full of the divine wisdom and the divine love".[2] Christ
was revealed therefore, not in a glorious body, but in flesh like
to sinful flesh, so as to destroy in his own flesh man's sin.
Original sin had not touched him, yet he accepted all the consequences of sin. "In his love, he nailed the sins of humanity
upon the tree, and, with his body, sin died ... Satan was con-
quered, for the innocent had suffered for the guilty. He who
rose from the dead was a *new* Man ... His obedience had won
for him the right to sit, even in his humanity, at God's right
hand ... The Son of man has become the Lord, the *Kyrios* ...
This God-Man transfigured and exalted in his glory as King,
Lord and High Priest, is the apogee of the whole New Testament Revelation."[3]

Christianity, then, is a mystery, because it is a revelation of
God to humanity; to the eye of faith it is a secret no longer.
And "at the heart of the Christian religion is a *sacrifice*, with

[1] p. 21 (references are to the French translation).   [2] p. 22.   [3] pp. 26-8.

the consecration which results from it: that of the God-Man dying on the cross and rising again for glory, and that of the Church following in his footsteps and in the power of the crucified God-Man, and finding divinisation in the sacrifice of the Lord ... The Church appropriates *his* sacrifice, and, transfigured in Christ's glory, rises with him from this world to God ... It is only by taking an active part in the actions of Christ that the Church *becomes* a living body, a *loving* Spouse". And Dom Casel quotes from Methodius's *Banquet of the Ten Virgins*: "the Church is, as it were, pregnant and in travail until Christ has taken form in us, until Christ is born in us, so that each of the saints, by his participation in Christ, becomes Christ".

"The Redemption, then", he continues, "must *be realized in us*. A mere 'application', while we remain in a purely passive attitude, is altogether insufficient ... it is a living and active part which we have to take in the redemptive work of Christ, a part which will be *passive*, certainly, in that Christ acts in us but also really *active* in that we are associated with this work by an action ... How is it possible to realize a work of such sublimity? ... The answer is given by our Lord, who has instituted for us the *mysteries of the Liturgy*, that is, the sacred actions which *we* perform but which our Lord (by the ministry of the Church's priests) realizes simultaneously in us. By these actions we can participate in the redemptive acts of Christ ... The mystery of Christ, which was accomplished in our Lord in all its historical and physical reality, is realized in us in symbol, beneath representative and figurative forms. Yet these are not mere appearances ... they communicate to us the full reality of the new life which Christ our Mediator offers to us. This altogether special sort of participation in Christ's life, which is both presented beneath the expression of a symbol and at the same time really effected, was called by the first Christians *mystic* participation". This time it is Cyril of Jerusalem who provides the illustration in his Second Mystagogic Catechism (he is speaking of our incorporation into Christ by Baptism); "Christ was crucified in actual fact, he was buried, and he really rose again: and of all this he has made us a gift so that *by participation in the imitation of his Passion* we should really obtain salvation. In you it is the resemblance of his Passion and Death which has taken place, and yet you have received the reality of salvation, and not only the resemblance".[1]

There we have the picture in outline. But, if we are to understand sufficiently the *centrality* of Christ, we must to some extent fill it out. First, then, Christ has reconciled humanity with his Father, and in doing so has brought back out of its slavery to the devil the inanimate creation, which depends upon man. So we find in the Eastern Liturgies the first part of the Eucharistic prayer, the Preface, expatiating with the greatest magnificence of language upon the *cosmic* character of Christ's work. All creatures, St Paul tells us, are "recapitulated" in Christ. "God perfected the unity of his work", writes Père Bouyer, "beyond all that any created spirit could foresee, by recapitulating it entirely in himself, gathering into his own Word made flesh all that created multiplicity of images of the uncreated Image".[2]

We are thus led to dwell, secondly, on the Word as the Father's Image. The Father gives his divine nature, in a giving which cannot be other than absolute, to the Son, in whom he is expressed. The Father is the giver, the Son the receiver, of the Godhead. And the Son, again in Père Bouyer's words, "lives only in returning to his beginning, one with him in the common spiration of their single love, which is the Holy Spirit". So we may speak of a divine and eternal "eucharist" in the literal sense, for God the Son finds his glory only in giving it back to God the Father. His incarnate life is simply a "temporal extension of a divine state of the begotten Word".[3] This mystery of divine generosity is the great secret of the Godhead which Christ came to reveal to us. The Christian Mystery is the mystery of our assumption with Christ, according to our created measure, into the divine life. We must pause, then, for a moment or two at least, to consider what that life is. How can we bring home to ourselves in some degree the ineffable and strictly incomprehensible love of the Father for the Son whereby the Son is the object of his infinite good-pleasure, not only the crown but the very *raison d'être* of all creation, in whose image

[1] pp. 29-33.
[2] *The Paschal Mystery* (*Le Mystère Pascal*), p. 80. (References are to the translation published by the Henry Regnery Company of Chicago.)
[3] *Op. cit.* pp. 108-9.

all things were made? We cannot expect to get very far at this
stage when we are only on the threshold of the Mystery. But we
can perhaps prepare ourselves, take some bearings.

Our Lord first *taught* his disciples about the gift which he was
about to bestow upon them, the gift of his Spirit; and when that
gift had been received, they saw in its light a fuller significance
in his words. We too must enter into the Mystery with his words
in our minds, be guided into the Mystery by them; and then
there will be an interaction between them and our life of prayer,
the life which begins with faith, the gateway to our eternal life
(for the knowledge of Jesus Christ, St John tells us, is *already*
eternal life while we are still on this earth). We must both begin
and end with the words of Christ. The mystic still needs the support of created analogies, although without faith he cannot
realize that the analogies are *true*. And he has received the gift of
faith by way of them. That is to say, that self-communication of
God himself which comes to him and sets God's own seal upon
the truths of faith gives him indeed an awareness of *God* in his
action upon the soul, a super-sensible awareness therefore, an
intellectual union with God, obscure but certain, so showing
him something of the inner meaning of Christ's words; yet he
must listen first of all to the words of the Gospel, because by
them his mind is opened to the new light. No man comes to
Christ unless the Father draws him. But, again, no man comes
to the Father save through Christ.

Thus it seems right that we should approach the mystery by
recalling Christ's supreme witness in the seventeenth chapter of
St John's Gospel:

That they may all be one, as thou, Father, in me, and I in
thee; that they also may be one in us: that the world may
believe that thou hast sent me. And the glory which thou hast
given me, I have given to them; that they may be one as we
also are one. I in them, and thou in me: that they may be
made perfect in one: and the world may know that thou hast
sent me and hast loved them, as thou hast also loved me.
Father, I will that where I am, they also whom thou hast
given me may be with me: that they may see my glory which
thou hast given me, because thou hast loved me before the

creation of the world. Just Father, the world hath not known thee: but I have known thee. And these have known that thou hast sent me. And I have made known thy name to them, and will make it known: that the love wherewith thou hast loved me may be in them, and I in them.

"The love wherewith thou hast loved me", "the glory which thou hast given me", "thou, Father in me, and I in thee"—we must think, then, of a Father and a Son who differ in nothing save that one is the Father and the other the Son. Our Lord is asking us to think of our familiar human relationships and to carry them upward to the final point at which they threaten to disappear altogether—but at that point there is to be not a disappearance, but a revelation. Then we shall *know*, in the dark knowledge of faith, that Christ and his Father are one, that he who has seen Christ has seen the Father. And this is inexpressible. But we can speak of the perfection of love which would belong to a society of persons who were not sundered from one another by the least shadow of misunderstanding, the smallest difference of temperament or habits or mental outlook, who lived simply for one another, delighting in one another's good without the slightest hint of selfishness. Yet these are *perfectly distinct* persons. How else would there be a life of love? The perfectly beloved must be the perfectly "not-I". Perfect distinction and perfect unity must be reconciled somehow in the end. And we begin to see, even in this distant approach to the Mystery, how the created universe, an echo or overflow of that generosity which is the very life of God, suggests to us this law by which variety and unity, richness and simplicity, go hand in hand.

"Thou has loved me before the creation of the world". The Father's gift to the Son is infinite; everything is for him. And the humanity of the Son is, as St Thomas puts it, the "instrument", the "conjoined instrument", of the Divinity. It is really his in such sort that the acts performed by means of it are the acts of the Word, of the Second Person of the Blessed Trinity, of God. We cannot think, therefore, that the Father's infinite good pleasure stops short, as it were, at the eternal Word and does not embrace the Word Incarnate. Here we have to remember

how easily those who have been brought up in ignorance of
the Gospel—which means nowadays our next-door neighbours
—utterly misconceive the words which are so often on our lips:
"the Word was made flesh". To them it seems as though these
words must mean that the Word, the Son of God, suffered some
mysterious degradation when he took to himself our human
nature and became Son of Man. This, then, again, is the
Christian Mystery: that there should be a union of God with
man such that although man is raised in Christ to this personal
identity with God, yet man should be still man and God be still
God—and we must add at once that it was for *us*, created
human persons, that the Incarnation took place, for us to
become, through Christ's natural sonship, God's adopted sons.
Is it, then, only as a means to an end that the humanity of
Christ is the object of the Father's good-pleasure? In reading
the records of Christian antiquity we might be moved to ask that
question, so great is the insistence of the Fathers upon the
Church, the Mystical Body, as the whole purpose of God's
creation. Until the final union with the Word takes place,
Christ, they even say, is *incomplete*. But at that point we realize
that we have misconstrued their language. Its very vigour in
asserting the truth has put us off the track. It is because we are
nothing without Christ that we are to be at last simply Christ:
it is because of the unity of Christians with Christ that Christ
without the Church would be Christ no longer. We are to be so
joined to the Incarnate Word that to speak of him is at the same
time to speak of us. By a Mystery which in its own way echoes
the Mystery of the hypostatic union, the union of the divine and
human natures in the Word, *Christ* means not only that union
of personal identity between God and man but the union of
grace between human persons and God in Three Persons,
which amounts, after all, to St Paul's "You are Christ's, and
Christ is God's".

The Fathers' refusal to consider the Incarnation apart from
the salvation of human beings does not entitle us to say that
they gave any answer to the question first brought into prominence by Duns Scotus: would the Incarnation have happened had
there been no sin? They were not given to speculative questions
of this nature, and many people would be inclined to say that

this was a good thing. In the case of our "elevation to the supernatural order" I would ask leave to agree. We need not ask:
"but what if God had chosen not to elevate us?" But in the
other case I am not sure. It seems to me that if we really believe
in human freedom (and the Fathers, faced by the philosophies
of their time, had to insist on it rather as we have to do nowadays) it is difficult to avoid thinking of "might-have-beens".
Adam—and Judas—might *not* have sinned. We cannot say
what would have happened instead ... but it would have made a
great difference. Anyhow to pursue this line of thought for a
little will lead us to consider more closely another feature of the
outline which we borrowed from Dom Casel: the destruction of
man's sin in the flesh of Christ.

But first I should like to combat the notion that controverted
questions of this kind are of no concern to any but professional
theologians. Theology has become a specialized study in recent
centuries as it was not before, and this, although perhaps inevitable, has been a bad thing for both clergy and laity. The
clergy have to some extent lost touch with the layman's mind,
and the layman has felt that he has no competence in the theological field. In certain parts of that field obviously he has none.
But the economy of our Redemption is the concern of all of us.
Clear thinking and scholarship are not the monopoly of the
clergy; and in this particular case it would seem to be largely a
question of the former. I do not propose to set out the arguments of Scotus over against those of St Thomas nor do I even
wish to recommend them. All I would say is that if you happen
to find it easier to accept Scotus's conclusion as part of your
theological thinking rather than St Thomas's you are perfectly
entitled to do so. It is an eminently respectable conclusion, and
in our day it seems to be gaining ground. Scotus's conclusion
that the Incarnation would have happened even if there had
been no sin controverts that of St Thomas, according to which
we are not entitled to go beyond the data of Scripture and
tradition—we know that Christ did come to save us from our
sins and there we must leave it. That sounds sensible enough.
But the difficulty seems to arise that if we do leave it there we
are committed to regarding the Incarnation as a sort of after-
thought on God's part, not of course in a temporal but in a

logical sense. For on this view it was only because he foresaw man's sin that God willed to send us his Son. The Church is the result of something which need not have happened, which God did not *intend* to happen; in fact, we may say, a sort of accident. It is true that on any showing God from all eternity saw the Incarnate Word as the Head of all creation—but only, on this view, because of man's sin. I hope I am not being unfair to the Thomist case. It is difficult to give a fair treatment of a case which one does not accept. But I am not trying to secure a verdict from you. I am only anxious on the one hand to avoid any suggestion that man's sin is a *positive* part of God's providence, that is, that it was necessary for Adam's sin—and Judas's—to take place,[1] and on the other to retain without qualifications or conditions the doctrine that Christ in his Mystical Body is the ultimate *raison d'être* of the whole creation.[2] It remains on any view that we cannot see how God could have shown his love to us in a more marvellous way than by the death of his Son.

That opens a fresh enquiry: *how* was this death our redemption? Here the Fathers seem only to increase the difficulties which we begin to face, for they speak of the payment of a debt, owed rather, it would seem, to the devil than to God. But even those who use this sort of language most consistently cannot be denying that the devil's power is subject to God's, so that there can be no serious question of God's paying him in a literal sense. The Fathers, indeed, also used another image, strictly irreconcilable with the first, which shows how little precision they attached to either: the devil, they also said, so far from receiving a due payment, was tricked into accepting the bait which was offered him, and, seizing upon the innocent, was justly deprived even of the guilty, his legitimate prey. To take this at its face-value would be ridiculous. But it would be rash to ridicule the Fathers for saying it. When you are dealing with a mystery, it is perhaps safer to use nursery language about it,

---

[1] When the *Exultet* on Holy Saturday uses this language about Adam's sin, we are not to take it, presumably, in a strict and absolute sense.

[2] When the purpose of creation is described as the "external glory of God" we must not think that God is supposed to be acquiring some "accidental" gain, for we can give him, strictly speaking, nothing at all. God wills the manifestation of himself—but not for himself, for us. God needs nothing, and is the end to which all things return. That sums up Christian teaching on this matter.

which should deceive nobody, than to give the impression by a concatenation of syllogisms that you have "explained" the whole thing. A mystery is an invitation to think, but you never get to the end of it. You can remove apparent contradictions by making the appropriate distinctions, but you will not necessarily find out much about it by that method. What the Fathers are trying to make us realize here by their use of this language is that Redemption is the work of God and that he freed us from the slavery of sin at a great price. Here I cannot do better than quote again from Père Bouyer: "The 'debt to the devil' and the 'debt to God' are in the last analysis simply two complementary aspects of the resistance to our future liberty which is set up in us in permanent fashion by the reality of our past liberty. God himself could not attenuate the tragic reality of this resistance without reducing our reality as free beings. The sinner will become just once more only when he has consummated the offering of himself *in the state in which his sin has placed him* and in no other. For sin has made us mortals, beings who must die, by a physical necessity—this is the debt to the devil, to whom we freely bound ourselves and whom his sin (irreparable, unlike ours) drags ineluctably to death. At the same time death is a moral necessity for us—this is the debt to God, whom we have freely rejected, making ourselves unworthy of the life which he gave us. So it would be to break the continuity between the sinners who we once were and the justified ones who we have now become if we were not brought out of sin into loving obedience through the gates of death. But the loving obedience brought into our mortal state and coinciding with all its painful reality transforms it, when the assimilation is complete, into a state of justice re-won and so of life regained—that is the trapping of the devil and the victory over him. The Cross, the act of self-forgetful love, will repair the Fall, the act of egoism—that is the satisfaction of God.

"And that is why the Lamb, who takes away the sins of the world, is the Lamb who was slain and why we are washed only in his blood ...

"The Just One suffered and died to redeem us, because only he could give our sufferings and our death the value of a sacrifice. But it is for us that he has offered it and we can make its fruits our own. In his incarnation he took upon himself all our humanity in potency; he brings it into himself in actuality by the Eucharist, more generally by the whole sacramental liturgy, of which the Eucharist is the centre and the source, pre-eminently the Paschal liturgy. He died *for us* at the first Christian Easter, he can and must die *in us* at each new Easter, through the Eucharistic Sacrament, the sacrament of Easter."[1]

But we may still ask: *How* does the Cross repair the Fall? Here we must be content with a very brief indication of the lines of thought which some theologians offer us. We cannot offer as an explanation the necessity of giving back to God the honour and glory of which sin has deprived him. However much we may refine upon this notion, the fact remains that sin has not deprived God of anything. The need for satisfaction arises not on God's side but on ours. Our return to God involves the consecration of our whole lives to him; we cannot overlook the past. If we love God we shall need to repair our past, to make ourselves fit for him by undoing, so far as in us lies, our wrongdoing. On God's side the Redemption is simply the work of love. Satisfaction is not a condition which he imposes before he will pardon us. He pardons us in giving us Christ, who *is* our redemption. Nevertheless sin is a revolt against God, and is therefore called an offence against him. It attacks God's purposes, and therefore reparation is due from the sinner. It is the Church's teaching that he must offer satisfaction, and this is naturally described as being offered to God.

What, then, are we to say of God's justice? That it means something far more profound than legal or distributive or penal justice. What is just is what the wisdom and holiness of God requires, what is as it ought to be in conformity with that wisdom and holiness. St Thomas, in a remarkable passage,[2] says that mercy is a kind of fulfilling of justice (*quaedam justitiae plenitudo*). Justice, then, so far from being in conflict with love, proceeds from love and is identical with it. Suffering is *just* suffering when it is the way of our return to God. It is required in the last analysis not by God but by ourselves. And so when Christ suffered for us he was not returning to God

---

[1] *Op. cit.* p. 201 and p. 208. I use here the translation published in *The Downside Review*, April 1948.

[2] *S. Th.* I, q. 21, a. 3, ad. 2.

something of which sin had deprived him. He suffered because in taking to himself our humanity he took to himself, *out of his limitless love for us*, that condition of disorder which is the consequence of sin. Christ's "satisfaction" is intelligible only if we consider his *union* with sinners, and theirs with him. He is not our *substitute* or even our ambassador. His "satisfaction" was made *on our behalf*, to our profit. And it is not *enough*, once more, to say that "his merits are imputed" to us. Until we look upon Christ the Redeemer as the Head of the Mystical Body we shall be in hopeless difficulties; only in the light of this doctrine can we think and talk profitably about his Passion and Death. The mystery of the Incarnation unites us *mystically* with him, and we have seen already to some extent what that should mean. What Christ does, we also *really* do in him. He unites us with that will to repair (not for himself but for us) what was and is his will, the will of Christ in the flesh; in so far as we are enabled to participate in him, *we* satisfy. But this we must *freely* do. We must accept his grace if it is to become *ours*. Thus to participate in his grace and to satisfy is one and the same.

We hear it said often enough that we could have been redeemed without the suffering of the Cross. This is a statement which can be understood in several senses. We might take it to mean that the Jewish rulers might *not* have rejected Christ. Or we might take it to mean (as it usually does) that Christ's satisfaction could have taken a form which would have involved less suffering for him; or that he need not have suffered at all. What are we to make of it in the light of the previous discussion? Certainly this: that Christ was not subject to an iron law of necessity, to some automatic impersonal system of compensation. The humanity of the Incarnate Word is the willing instrument of infinite and immutable love. There is in him the perfect correspondence of a human will with the Divine Will. But it seems misleading to say, as some theologians continue to do, that Christ received a special order from his Father that he must accept the death of the Cross as the price of our redemption. Such language may bear a tolerable interpretation, but it is hardly suitable, even if we go on to offer explanations—as that this death would manifest the horror of sin as well as love of

God in a unique fashion. There is the danger to which all commercial metaphors are exposed. And it is difficult to see what point there is in speaking of a "special" order. What happened surely was that Christ came into this world to lead a perfect human life—this and the wedding of his Spouse the Church, consummated in his death and resurrection, was that *work* of his to which he so often referred. He came to live *our* life and to live it as it ought to be lived, as a life of perfect obedience. Thus he would not save himself from the result of this encounter of his sinlessness with man's sinfulness, from the Cross.

This seems to give us the explanation of St Paul's statement that Christ "emptied himself". His human will embraced with joy the design of God's infinite mercy that he for our sakes should unite us to himself by taking *our* flesh, foregoing the privileges which in a sinless world would have flowed from the hypostatic union of the humanity with the divinity. He used his divine power for us, never for himself. And so when his work was accomplished, when his victory was won on Calvary and his triumph declared on the first Easter morning, it was, as the Fathers loved to repeat, from the pierced side of the new Adam that the new Eve sprang. If we add to these hastily drawn lines of approach to an inexhaustible mystery both Duns Scotus's hypothesis and an all-embracing view of the divine economy associated particularly with St Irenaeus, we see Christ as the centre of history, a centre which is nevertheless omnipresent, in whose image all things were made, by whom as well as in whom all things are fulfilled: before his Incarnation the "far-off event to which the whole creation moves", uniting with himself all God's lovers in every age, preparing his chosen people to receive him; in his first coming fulfilling the eternal purpose by which mankind was to see him in the flesh, to learn of God's hidden life from human lips, to be mystically united with that life by means of that flesh—but, since sin had come into the world, only through suffering, Christ's suffering and ours: in his last coming the hope of his Church, present among us and yet always looked for, the Alpha and the Omega.

III

CHRIST'S SACRIFICE AND OURS

W E ARE INCORPORATED INTO CHRIST AT BAPTISM. BUT this incorporation is not an end in itself but the beginning of a new life, the life for which we were made. It is eternal life—on condition that we first live it in this world. The means by which this life is maintained and brought to maturity, the means too by which men are brought to it out of ignorance and sin, is the supreme Christian act, the offering of the Holy Sacrifice of the Mass.

What is a sacrifice? Various answers to this question have been given in the past by Catholic theologians and as a result there has been a good deal of confusion in the minds of the faithful. The writer whose account is to my mind the most satisfactory is Canon Eugène Masure, whose book *Le Sacrifice du Chef* I translated into English a few years ago (*The Christian Sacrifice*, Burns Oates and Washbourne). I think it may be safely said that his view is becoming more and more widely accepted, and I shall be doing little more than providing a rough statement of it in this chapter. The view is indebted to Père de la Taille's *Mysterium Fidei*, but it does not involve his conclusion that the Last Supper was only the pledge and the first stage, as it were, of the Sacrifice of Calvary, so that it was not (P. de la Taille's opponents would say) that same sacrifice offered in a different manner (the Council of Trent's description of the Mass), but only a part of it—in brief, that it was not the first *Mass*, Christ's presence in the sacred species being that of a victim only in so far as he was *pledged* to the sacrifice of Calvary. But there is one question of principle which must be considered before I proceed. It may be objected that I have begun with the wrong question. To ask: "what is a sacrifice?" may be considered an abstract form of approach which is unsuitable when we are dealing with the unique, with that climax of history which explains sacrifice and is not itself to be explained by it. It is true that Christ's sacrifice is the perfect sacrifice, that the meaning of sacrifice is not fully seen except in the light of the Christian Revelation. But it is also surely true that Christ does not destroy when he fulfills. The law of sacrifice is a law of human nature at all times. And if we are to approach the text of the Missal with a proper understanding, we must first take care that we have cleared our minds of the false notions of sacrifice which have been so much to the fore in recent centuries.[1]

At the beginning of this century sacrifice was commonly defined by Catholic writers as the offering to God of some sensible object by a legitimate priest and its immolation (understood as some kind of destruction), in order to recognize God's sovereignty over all things and to win pardon for sins. The parts of this definition were thought of as being all of them essential to the whole; thus sacrifice (and so religion itself) was bound up with sin, and some kind of annihilation was supposed to be involved in sacrifice as its material element, for only so could God receive due honour. This way of approaching the question involves a pessimism and a superficial view (to give it no worse name) of our duties towards God; and it easily implies a false view of God's own nature. Sacrifice, properly understood, is something positive, which springs from our deepest needs, from the very roots of human personality.

The principle which lies behind all sacrifice is found in St Augustine's famous sentences: "Visible sacrifice is the sacrament of the invisible sacrifice (of our inward religious life), that is, its sacred sign. ... Any work performed that we may cleave to God in holy union is a true sacrifice."[2] Sacrifice, in the accepted sense, is always visible; but it is always a sign of the invisible. In the *Summa Theologica* St Thomas adopts the second passage from St Augustine as a general formula.[3] Quoting the first passage he adds "therefore everything that is presented (*exhibetur*) to God that the spirit of man may be lifted up to him may be called a sacrifice",[4] and this does seem to show his mind quite clearly, although when he goes on to detail three reasons for sacrifice (turning to our present condition) he places the remission of sins and the preservation of grace before union with

---

[1] In what follows on Sacrifice in general I draw on an article published in *The Clergy Review* of June 1944.
[2] *De Civ. Dei*, Bk. x, chs. 5 and 6.   [3] II, II, q. 85, a. 3, ad. 1.
[4] III, q. 22, a. 2.

God. This same Augustinian definition is paraphrased in the *Summa contra Gentiles*[1] where St Thomas adds that the soul (*mens*) offers itself to God in sacrifice "as to the principle of its creation, the author of its operation and the end of its beatification" (repeated in substance in the greater *Summa*, II, II, q. 85, a. 2.). To clinch the matter we have the following passage on the Old Law: "Sacrifices put before men's eyes the right ordering of the mind to God ... man must recognize that all things that he has come to him from God ... and he must refer them to him as their last end."[2]

It is in the light of these passages that we must interpret the following: "there is sacrifice properly so called when the things which are offered to God are the subject of an action, as when animals were killed and burnt and when bread is broken and eaten and blessed. This is the meaning of the word itself; sacrifice means *making sacred* ... oblation is a common name for everything presented to God's service ... if anything is [so] presented to be transformed into something sacred ... then we have both oblation and sacrifice".[3] "Transformed" represents *consumendum*, which sounds like special pleading only if we forget the context.[4] Sacrifice, then, for St Thomas, is primarily a transformation.

We may conclude that a sacrifice is an object made sacred and that to sacrifice is to provide oneself with such a sacred object. The writer of the article "Sacrifice", in the *Dictionnaire de Théologie Catholique* (1939) writes as follows: "The theory of sacrifice-destruction is (relatively) recent and without sufficient foundation; that of sacrifice-oblation, on the other hand, is guaranteed by the witness of the Fathers and theologians".[5] The same writer quotes[6] a passage from a book by M. Lepin[7] which may conveniently sum up our general results so far: "Man's adoration will not lead him any more than his sin to annihilate the being which he has received, as if this were the best means of honouring the divine Being. His most deep-seated tendency will be rather to bear witness that he receives

---

[1] Bk. III, ch. 120.   [2] I, II, q. 102, a. 3.   [3] II, II, q. 85, a. 3, ad 3; q. 86 c.
[4] M. Lepin in his great book *L'Idée du Sacrifice de la Messe*, seems to have made out his case for this translation (he sees a reference here to the bread of the Eucharist).
[5] Col. 678.   [6] Col. 675.   [7] *La Messe et Nous*, 1937.

his being from his Creator, and to offer it in a movement of desire and intention and effective determination to him who is its last end, as he is its first beginning. This is the only way, glorious to God, of recognizing his sovereign sway. Man's sacrifice will not be an act of destruction separating the creature violently from his Creator, but an act of *offering* or *donation* which opens the way to intimate communion with him."

At this point we must consider more closely the function of *signs*. In the first place, the outward sign of our inward religion, the liturgical rite, is not just a piece of pious make-believe. It belongs to the very essence of the rational animal that he should express himself in sensible forms. Not only does his religion demand to be "translated" externally by a psychological necessity, but also, as we have seen, it is itself engendered by this expression. We are familiar with the idea of the spiritual coming down to us in a material envelope. We are less familiar with the idea of making the material the vehicle by which our worship and love of God, all our hopes and fears, may rise to him. Yet, as we have also seen, it is the peculiar business of man, corresponding with his peculiar position in the scheme of things, to saturate matter with spirit—to give it *significance*. And it is by becoming thus incarnate, following the law of our nature, that our desire of God becomes effective. Such is our way to God, and, apart from this, sacrifice is meaningless.

But sacrifice aims at something more than a mere stimulus on the way to God. It aims at union with him. We make *something* sacred, and we believe that God accepts it. Once accepted by him, it is the means by which his blessings come down to us, the channel of our communion with him, the pledge of our heavenly alliance and the foretaste of our future blessedness. The sign of our religion becomes the sign of his grace. When we look back at the strange medley of rites in ancient sacrifice, so unintelligible at first and sometimes so revolting, we can discern the same rhythm in all of them, "the hidden line of movement towards God".[1] What, then, more precisely, is the inner logic of this undertaking? We are on the way to God, and we must express (and so expand) our longing to behold him; at the same time we hope to gain some earnest of our distant prize. We

---

[1] Canon Masure's expression.

would show in some way our desire to throw ourselves upon him, to count the world well lost to gain him; so we make over effectively to his service some gift which he has made us, some visible object of his creation. We give it its true significance. If it is in our power and belongs to us, that is only because both we and it belong to God. It is a stepping-stone to God, and we express by a deliberate ritual act our recognition of this. We offer ourselves with it that God may ratify it by his acceptance and return it to us; it goes on embassy from us, and it comes back laden with heavenly wealth. But that involves a preliminary renunciation. We must set it aside, deprive ourselves of the use of it for any lesser end. This is immolation.

The coming of sin gives immolation a fresh emphasis. Let us consider how sin came. God asked our first parents for a sign. A certain tree was set aside; they were to forgo the use of it at God's command. The metaphysic of sacrifice, its essential law, was set before them, and they disobeyed it. Henceforth sin sweeps us from our course, the course which God had planned for us, upward and not free from danger, but unbroken. And now a further and a previous means of union is required— breaking with sin. Not only must we recognize that this world's goods are God's and that we must not rest in them; we must recognize too that we are chained to them and we must break our chains. That is why the "giving up" in sacrifice, the immolation, may become destruction. Sacrifice must symbolize now a bitter necessity, an uprooting, a doing violence to ourselves. The law of sacrifice, then, is the law of our return to God. And Christ, in becoming man, placed his human nature under it. Christ's return to his Father, apart from the conditions which sin brought into the world, would have been nothing but the perfect offering or opening of himself, the absolute welcoming of his Father's love, without sorrow or pain. In the conditions which sin brought into the world Christ's sacred humanity was at the mercy of the world's disorder. The complete reciprocity between his will and his Father's will meant that he must lead back to the Father the race of which he is the Head at any cost, even by the death of the Cross. The charity of Christ conquers even death. *Christus vincit*! His perfect offering began with his birth, triumphed in his death, and triumphs now in heaven and upon our altars. The Cross does not increase the union of the Son with the Father; nothing could increase it. But it causes Christ's worship of his Father to issue in a *visible* offering—that is in sacrifice strictly so-called. Thus we may see in the Resurrection and the Ascension the ratification of Christ's offering, the visible acceptance of it, its second and glorious phase—for sacrifice, as we know it, has always these two sides to it, the first provisional and sorrowful, the second definitive, an apotheosis. Too often the Resurrection is not in practice that centre of devotion which the Church's Liturgical Year would make it. Every Sunday, in the Church's year, is a little Easter.

The words which we translate "sacrifice" and "oblation" in the Epistles of St Paul and St John are words which refer not only to Christ's death but to Christ himself. The inspired writers are looking at sacrifice not only as an action but as a thing,[1] more precisely as something acted upon. So Christ himself is the perfect sacrifice. In him is found all that the ancient sacrifices foreshadowed. He has fulfilled and abolished them. He has put his whole human nature into his sacrifice. The patriarch of old gave his possessions; Christ gave himself. The priest and the victim here and here only are one and the same.

It must be the one ambition of sinful man to become incorporated into Christ, to free himself from sin and go through Christ to God. Are we then just to turn our minds to Christ and enter into a spiritual communion with him? Is all outward showing of our love and worship abrogated by his perfect sacrifice? Is there no sign, no visible guarantee, of the new life which his death has brought us? The Council of Trent put the answer to all these questions in the following words: "After celebrating the ancient Pasch, which the children of Israel immolated in memory of their coming forth from Egypt, our Saviour constituted himself the new Pasch to be immolated by the Church under sensible signs through the ministry of priests, in memory of his passage from this world to the Father, when by the shedding of his blood he rescued us from the power of darkness to lead us to his Kingdom." Christ made himself our sacrifice by taking bread and wine and uttering the words of consecration: "This is my Body: this is the Chalice of my Blood".

[1] This explains apparent inconsistencies in the account *supra*.

This bread and this wine are to be the *signs* of Christ, signs which convey what they signify. Human signs convey reality imperfectly, divine ones perfectly. The bread and wine, beneath their appearances, become Christ himself. Christ, to perpetuate his sacrifice for us, places his whole reality beneath a sign. The sacrifice of the Mass is the sign or sacrament of Christ's sacrifice, the sacrament of the Redemption.

We have seen how man incarnates his worship and saturates with it the world of matter. Christ, following the law of nature and ministering to our human needs,[1] solves the problem which his perfect sacrifice had seemed to raise. Sacrifice seemed to have ended with his death; it seemed to annihilate itself in its final triumph. But he has given us his sacrifice under a sacrament so that we too may sacrifice. We enter into his sacrifice; *our* bread and wine actually become it. Through that sacrifice, which is himself, we are incorporated into him. When we receive the Holy Eucharist, the sacrament of man's worship, transubstantiated into the sacrament of his Redemption, is now the sacrament of the new life. Sacrifice is for union; Christ, our sacrifice, unites us with himself. Christ's simple action of taking bread and wine was thus the means of giving us his supernatural life, and also of giving us a sacrifice—a liturgical sacrifice. There was no liturgy on Calvary; but by his institution of the previous evening Christ put his whole reality at our disposal beneath a rite—and one which was to represent his death. "This is the chalice of my Blood of the New Testament". And St Paul says that "we show forth the Lord's death until he come". All the reality of Christ is there. He comes to us in the Mass as the consummated sacrifice, the Lamb who once was slain and who is now in glory. Christ gave us in this same simple action the perfect Eucharist or thanksgiving, for our sacrifice becomes Christ's sacrifice, that is, Christ himself, and the pledge of the eternal banquet when we shall see him face to face without the veil of sacrament.

But a question arises: What more precisely is meant by saying that Christ is immolated in the Mass? We immolate Christ, St Thomas tells us, because in the Mass we become sharers of the fruit of the Lord's Passion,[2] and he quotes from one of the

---

[1] *Sicut humana natura exigit* (the Council of Trent).   [2] *S. Th.*, III, 83, 1.

secret prayers in the Missal:[1] "whenever the commemoration of this victim is made, the work of our redemption is set in motion". In the Mass, the Redemption is *applied* to us; this is the language of Trent. Christ's immolation operates on us, and we draw upon it. The Mass is the means by which its virtue redeems us, giving us life. There is no need to read more into "immolation" than "sacrificial offering", and the Missal uses it in this general sense. Turn to the prayers for the Masses of the Saints in the month of June and you will find several cases of it. We offer Christ, then, by our own sacrificial action, in that our bread and wine, by his institution, become himself, his sacrifice. The butchery of Calvary is not repeated; but the love which was the substance of Christ's life, focussed on Calvary, is focussed still in his life of glory and on our altars. Through our external act, under the visible forms of our own offerings, it is still offered by Christ in a true, real sacrifice. He is unchanged, but he changes our offerings into himself. Through us, Christ offers himself for us.

We must now notice that St Thomas has proposed another explanation, in the article just quoted, of Christ's immolation in the Mass. "The celebration of the sacrament", he here tells us, "is a representative image of Christ's Passion, which is his true immolation. ... And so [it] is called Christ's immolation." And he quotes St Augustine, who draws a parallel: when we see someone's picture, we say "that's so-and-so". This is quite true, no doubt, so far as it goes. But, as it stands, it does not do much to explain *how* Christ's immolation is found in the Mass. In many popular books a false emphasis is laid on this aspect of symbolic representation, and writers point to the separate consecrations of the bread and the wine, seeing in this that "destructionist immolation" which they deem requisite for a true sacrifice. It is only a "mystical immolation", they some-times tell us, but our action does bear directly on the Body of Christ in the first consecration and on his Blood in the second. In *fact* (it is admitted) they cannot be separated from one another; but there is some sort of distinction between them, some sort of separation, even if in a mere logical sense. Or, in another version, the separate species of bread and wine give to

[1] For the 9th Sunday after Pentecost.

the Mass a sacrificial character by *symbolizing* Christ's death. Here is a very different view of sacrifice from that which has been put forward in this chapter.

A few more words must be said about the opposing theory mentioned in the last paragraph. It is often derived, consciously or unconsciously, from a counter-Reformation tradition in Catholic theology, which we may be permitted to criticize. Controversy with Protestants led many Catholics into extreme positions. In their efforts to show that the Mass *is* a real sacrifice, they evolved theories which postulated some effect on our Lord, some fresh immolation, something additional to his immolation on Calvary. "Immolation" was taken to mean, if not some kind of destruction, at least some kind of change which should be equivalent or approximating to it. Thus a reduction of Christ's glorified state was sometimes proposed as a true solution. Even when this was seen to be out of the question—it is a monstrous notion—the consumption of the Sacred Species was put forward as an alternative means of solution by other theorists. The whole debate was controlled by a too narrow conception. The deepest sense of sacrifice was no longer realized. This played into the hands of the "Reformers". For the Mass is not, on these theories, the self-same sacrifice as that of Calvary. According to these it is not enough that it draws on Calvary, reaping its fruits: it must add something to Christ's own offering of his sacrifice; he must somehow repeat it.

The Mass is, in truth, complete as a sacrifice. But it is our sacrifice which Christ takes over—by which his own takes body. And it is *relative* to his absolute sacrifice of Calvary. The relation between the Mass and the Cross is, then, the relation between the sign and that which it signifies. "Signifies" does not mean "symbolizes" here. It means to "re-present" in the sense of "make really present". Christ is made really present, and it is *he* who is our sacrifice. Into his sign Christ puts the entire Redemptive mystery, not only his Passion and Death, but his Resurrection and his Ascension. This does not mean that there is some re-enactment of the events of Christ's earthly life:[1] it means that we have our Lord in all his reality in his consummated but ever-active glorious state. The past is not repeated,

[1] As Dom Casel's view is held to imply by many critics.

but it is not dead: it remains real in the present. In Christ's continuing love, in which we are caught up at Mass, all his earthly triumphs are concentrated.[1] His sign at the Last Supper and his sign on the Cross perfectly expressed and contained what they signified. The Cross was the sign of his boundless love. His Sacrifice at the Last Supper was the sign or sacrament of this sign,[2] containing already the fruits of the Cross. There are still ideas about the Mass in the minds of the faithful which have a flavour of the *macabre*. This is all wrong. The Mass is the memorial of the Cross; it shows us our sins. But it is always a triumph—the triumph of the new life.

This is the crown of the whole sacramental system, of the whole spiritual organization which seems so complex until we see the key to it. The growth of supernatural life in ourselves and others is the one final aim of all our prayers and actions. Everything prepares for this and gains its meaning from it. This was the purpose of Christ's life—to give us the means of union with God which God's wisdom chose for us. But to attain this union we have to enter into his sacrifice. We have indeed a part to play. We have God's guarantee at Mass that the fruits of Calvary are there for us to draw on, that Christ is there to feed us with himself. And only by conforming ourselves to him, to his sacrifice, shall we find his presence in our souls in its full operation. Christ comes to us; but we must *use* his presence.

Two powers are put at our disposal in the Mass-Sacrifice: the power of Christ, our sacrifice, present on the altar, ready to pour through all the world to right its wrongs, to give us strength against sin, to lead us past every obstacle; and the power of his presence in our souls in Holy Communion. This is

[1] But this does not mean that the historical event of Christ's offering on Calvary continues, as those would appear to say who assert the 'numerical identity' between that offering and the offering of the Mass-Sacrifice.

[2] These "signs" are properly so called because in each case the visible is the expression or "container" of the invisible. But it will be obvious that it is not in precisely the same sense that our offerings "contain" our worship, that Christ's Passion and Death "contained" his love and that the consecrated elements "contain" Christ's Body and Blood. When this is realized, we may safely sum up by saying that, by our repetition of Christ's sign at the Last Supper, our sign becomes the sign of the whole Christian Mystery. This last use of the word "sign" in the sense of "sacrament" has fallen into some disuse as a way of referring to the Real Presence as a result of controversies with Protestants who used "sign" in the sense of "*empty* sign". Such expressions as the "sacramental world" are also, perhaps, misleading in this connexion; what *becomes present* is not a "sacramental Christ" but the whole reality of Christ.

the reservoir of spiritual energies; the time of Mass is in a quite literal sense infinitely precious, for the reservoir itself is infinite. There is no limit to what we may draw from it. It rests with us. Catholics have not always been clear about their part in the Mass. Because the greatest act in the world, the transubstantiating act, happens whether or no we all fix our attention on it, it does not follow that we are just to stand and wait developments. Quite on the contrary, it is precisely as the most tremendous opportunity for our own efforts that we should look at it. The priest alone is empowered to repeat Christ's words and so to perform the sacrament of his sacrifice; but we all "immolate": the sacrifice is ours. Our offering at Mass, which is also our preparation for Communion, must be the dedication of ourselves to all God's purposes, the total offering of ourselves to him, the imitation of Christ's charity. For this very charity is to pour upon us from Christ himself, God with us, if we are ready to receive it. To sum up our present matter, then, Holy Communion has its supreme value because it is the Communion of the Christian *Sacrifice*. The sacrifice has its inexhaustible value because it *is* Christ—and Christ comes to give himself to us in *Communion*. There can be no effective communion without sacrifice. And sacrifice always looks forward to communion. Holy Communion is not a private devotion. We are all familiar with that statement. But how easy it is to forget what it implies! Holy Communion joins us together, if we will only make *use* of it, into the only indissoluble union, the bond of Christ. This is the only solution of human conflicts which strikes down to the roots of things.

When we feel discouraged about ourselves, we can, perhaps, make the following test of our progress: do we, in spite of dullness and dryness, realize more that the Mass *is* the centre? Have we a greater *desire* to offer ourselves and to receive God's gifts? If we can answer "Yes", then, in spite of our faults, and in spite of our feelings, we are in the right way. Complacency is a very great evil. But so is worry—especially worry about our spiritual states. If we have learnt the meaning of sacrifice, in other words, if we are really wanting God, we must brush aside discouragement as a temptation. If we live the Mass, if we make our lives a sacrifice, we shall have suffering no doubt as well as joy. But we shall have joy, here as well as hereafter. And always, even in suffering, we shall have peace.

In conclusion something must be said about the Eucharistic symbolism. According to our account, it is not because the Mass is the memorial of Christ's Sacrifice of Calvary that it is the Christian Sacrifice but because it is *Christ acting upon us* under the sign of our own sacrificial offering. The liturgical rite with bread and wine seems to show us one magnificent shifting image: of ourselves in our offerings, of the Body and Blood of Christ our sacrifice, and of our incorporation into him. We should therefore suppose that this is the essential symbolism of the Eucharist. But the Mass *is* the memorial of Christ's Sacrifice of Calvary. Must not Calvary itself be symbolized in it? It is maintained by most modern writers, whatever their views may be about the essence of sacrifice in general or the essence of the Christian Sacrifice in particular, that the separation of the species at Mass *symbolizes* the separation of Christ's Body and Blood on Calvary. The explanation does not appear to have any definite Patristic support except for a passage of St Gregory Nazienzus; it seems to have become current along with the "destructionist" view of sacrifice,[1] and the portrayal of the *event* of Christ's death, of the actual *separating* of the Body from the Blood, does not seem a natural interpretation of what actually happens in the Mass (a *mime* of Christ's death, in any case, is not the sort of thing we should ordinarily call a symbol, which we think of rather as an analogue of what is symbolized than as a reproduction). But there is no conclusive reason why the explanation should not be a case of legitimate "development", as with the mixing of the wine with water, which has come to stand as a symbol for the hypostatic union or for the union of the faithful with Christ, or the symbolism of the grains of wheat in the single host and the grapes pressed into the one chalice, which has suggested to Christians from very early times the unity of the offerers.[2]

There is no difficulty about saying that the bread and wine, since they recall Christ's Body and Blood, recall also the

---

[1] Cf. Fr Joseph Kramp, S.J., *The Liturgical Sacrifice of the New Law*, Eng. Trans., Herder, 1927, pp. 107-10.
[2] This symbolism has been somewhat blown upon recently by Dom Capelle—unnecessarily, I think.

breaking of his Body and the shedding of his Blood.[1] Are not, then, these difficulties about the precise character of the symbolism trifling? Their importance is, I would say, that they lead us to ask the more far-reaching questions: are we to think of the Mass simply as the sacramental sacrifice of Calvary and to say that the rite must therefore symbolize *directly and essentially* Calvary? Or are we to think of it as the sacrifice of Calvary because it is the sacrament of the whole Christian mystery at the centre of which is Calvary? If we take the latter view, we shall find the memorial of Calvary present, indeed, but present within a context which, as a whole, will be the direct subject of the essential symbolism. In the course of chapters which follow evidence will be offered to show that the second alternative is indicated by the prayers of the Liturgy.[2]

[1] In the final pages of his impressive posthumous work, *La Théologie du Corps Mystique* (Desclée de Brouwer, 1946), P. Emile Mersch, S.J., stresses the indication of Christ's total abandonment made by his offering of himself under the species of bread and wine. Although P. Mersch has written what is probably the finest account in our time of the Mass as the Sacrament of Christ's *dying*, he refers to the symbolism of *separation* only in passing and remarks that it is recommended to us not by Christ's ceremony of institution but by the authority of theologians and by tradition.

[2] It will also become clearer that there is no question of a mere juxtaposition of Christ, as the consummated sacrifice, and our active sacrifice: his activity *enables* us to sacrifice as Christians. Cf. pp. 60-62 and Dom Sebastian Moore in *The Downside Review*, Autumn 1951.

IV

THE ORDINARY OF THE MASS : THE SYNAXIS AND THE OFFERTORY

THE LITURGICAL TEXTS, TO WHICH AT LAST WE NOW TURN, will be drawn almost entirely from the Roman Missal. Some principle of selection has to be employed, and, since the Missal is the only liturgical book which is regularly used by the faithful, the choice is an obvious one. But I should like to emphasize, in passing, once for all, that it would be a great pity if educated Catholics confined their attention exclusively to the Roman Missal. It is highly desirable that they should be acquainted at least to some extent not only with the baptismal Liturgy, the formularies for the administration of the other sacraments and the Divine Office (on which I shall touch only in the last chapter) but also with Eastern Liturgies (on which I shall hardly even touch); these Liturgies, as we are constantly reminded by such writers as Mr Donald Attwater and Mr Archdale King, are of the greatest value in themselves as impressive and illuminating monuments of Christian antiquity, and are the object of very special solicitude on the part of the Holy See, which has urged on many occasions the great spiritual loss which would ensue from allowing them to fall into disregard and desuetude.

It will be most convenient, I think, in beginning to consider the Ordinary of the Mass, to imagine that we are taking part in a *Missa Dialogata*, a Mass, that is to say, in which the congregation join with the celebrant in those prayers which are not specially reserved to him—not only in the responses given by the server in their name in the celebration of Low Mass, but also in all that is sung by the congregation or the choir at High Mass. It will be possible in this way to postpone certain problems of participation in the Liturgy and of liturgical reform to a later stage at which we shall be in a better position for dealing with them.

What follows has a severely practical purpose: simply to draw attention to certain features of the eucharistic Liturgy which seem to require special consideration from the participants, to underline or bring to a point elements of liturgical instruction which will be found easily enough in the abundant literature on the subject but which may be usefully grouped together here. A superficial acquaintance with the Roman rite will be presupposed, and it may be observed that there is no reason why a fairly complete understanding of it should not be presupposed in the case of intelligent Catholics since explanatory Missals are so readily obtainable and so obviously indispensable. This modest task of exposition has been lightened by the recent appearance of a little book by Fr John Coventry, S.J., *The Breaking of Bread* (Sheed and Ward), which has summarized the recent findings of liturgical scholarship, such as Fr Pius Parsch's book on the Mass and Fr Jungmann's monumental *Missarum Sollemnia* (it is illustrated by 63 excellent photographs of the principal actions of the Mass); but we shall be concerned with historical matters only in so far as they contribute to our practical purpose. It must be understood that some details in what follows are controverted by liturgical specialists and that there is no pretension here to liturgical scholarship.

Following Fr Coventry, I shall refer to the ante-Mass or first part of our present Roman Mass as the *Synaxis* to emphasize its continuity with the practice of the Jewish synagogue from which it sprang. It is essentially a service of instruction in the Scriptures and of preparatory prayer to which an Entrance Rite, now represented only by the Introit antiphon, was added later. It contains no references to the Christian Sacrifice (except in some modern Masses for particular days, that is to say in the variable parts of the Mass, and we are concerned at present only with the text of the invariable parts, reserving the special antiphons, prayers, lessons and prefaces for later treatment). The reason for that is shown by its more usual name "The Mass of the Catechumens". The *Synaxis*, nevertheless, does prepare the faithful for their great undertaking. The forty-second psalm, *Judica*, with which, nowadays, it begins at the foot of the altar does suggest to us the dispositions with which we should

approach the Holy Sacrifice, dispositions not only of supplication and humility but also of confidence and joy. The antiphon
speaks of our approach to the altar of God "who makes joyful
our youth", and the appropriateness of this reference to *youth*,
to spiritual joy, has often been emphasized.[1] This preparatory
psalm was of monastic origin; it was at one time to all intents
and purposes a part of the Divine Office, and in beginning and
ending with an antiphon it was simply conforming with the
usual rules of psalmody.

We may clear up the whole subject of antiphons once for all
by borrowing a paragraph from Fr Coventry (p. 59): "The
antiphon was a musical necessity, a verse of a psalm sung first
by the cantor to show what tune was going to be used before
the psalm itself was started (the use of musical instruments for
long being regarded as 'pagan'); two halves of the choir would
then, in the Office, sing the psalm answering each other verse by
verse. There is, however, an older type of psalmody which we
meet in the liturgy, Responsory singing: here a verse or versicle
(part of a verse) was sung by a cantor, repeated by everyone,
and again repeated by them after every verse of the psalm. This
goes right back to Jewish practice, and belongs to congregational singing before there was any semi-professional body to
take over (and perhaps monopolise) the chant. There would not
be 'books' to go round, and anyway people could not read; so
by this method the whole congregation could join in a psalm,
while only the cantor needed a book. Some of the psalms were
written to be sung this way, e.g. Ps. cxxxv which repeats 'for
his mercy endureth for ever' after every new phrase. It is
possibly in imitation of this type of singing that we find in
antiphonal singing the antiphon repeated at the end of the
psalm: it gave the congregation a chance to join in."

The fact that this particular psalm and antiphon (together
with the other prayers said at the foot of the altar) were not
added to the Liturgy of the Mass until the 16th century should
not deter us from benefiting from it. There is sometimes a

---

[1] Notably by Pierre Le Brun, the 18th-century Oratorian writer of whose
classical work *Explication de la Messe* Abbot Cabrol has said that it "still remains the best book written on the Mass". (*The Holy Sacrifice*, Burns Oates,
1937, p. 87)—a similar remark by Dom Henri Leclercq is quoted in a brief fore-
word to the recent edition of the book in the *Lex Orandi* series.

danger of a certain liturgical snobbery—of looking down (unconsciously) on "additions" to the Mass. There are anomalies in our existing Liturgy, as we shall see; a good many of them. But nothing is to be gained and a good deal would be lost by canonizing an arbitrarily selected stratum of the Liturgy, that (say) which could be broadly described as "patristic", and regarding everything else as intruded.

The *Confiteor* which follows emphasizes the corporate character of the rite in which we are engaged. It is a public act of repentance in which priest and people acknowledge their faults to one another—but not only to one another: we call in to witness and to intercede for us the whole host of heaven. We are now acting as members of a society of which only a small branch, so to say, is functioning on this planet at any one time; we may hope that most of it is in heaven. The text of the Liturgy frequently suggests that there is a close communication between earth and heaven, the angels not excluded, at Mass. The short dialogue which follows repeats the notes of joyful confidence and supplication (*et plebs tua laetabitur in te; ostende nobis Domine, misericordiam tuam*). And it ends with the first instance of the *Dominus Vobiscum*. This untranslatable summons is apt to seem a very perfunctory affair. Familiarity makes one forget that it *is* a summons; and here we have also an anomaly, for the priest does not turn to the congregation, as he normally does when he uses the formula on subsequent occasions to call their special attention to important stages in the function, to unite them with him in a particularly emphatic way (servers have a curious unwillingness to enunciate the final word of the response: *et cum spiritu tuo*).

The prayer *Aufer* which sums up what has preceded, a sort of collect as at the end of one of the hours of the Divine Office, is said silently by the priest as he goes up the altar-steps. If we ask with him for the forgiveness of our sins and for pure minds in our approach to the holy of holies, we shall probably find that he is beginning to read the Introit from the Missal by the time that we have finished (he is supposed to be in the Sacristy in less than half an hour from the time of leaving it, which in view of the various additions to the Mass is perhaps another anomaly). But we shall not have missed anything that directly concerns us: the intervening prayer is for the forgiveness of the priest's personal sins (ending with the singular possessive *mea*—a sign that it is not only a late insertion but, unlike the rest of the text so far, a late composition). It begins with a reference to the relics in the altar-stone, which the priest kisses—the occurrence of this gesture is worth looking out for in the sequel; it is an ancient token of love for Christ, whom the altar signifies, and it ought to be helpful to see the priest make it. We are not supposed to have our noses buried in our Missals all the time.[1]

The Introit presents us with a more startling anomaly. Originally it was a psalm sung to welcome the celebrant and his ministers and to accompany their procession to the sanctuary. This became established by the 5th century.[2] Now it consists only of an antiphon, a single verse of a psalm with *Gloria Patri*, and the antiphon repeated. This is one of the points at which it is forcibly brought home to us that Low Mass is a truncated form of High Mass. At Low Mass it is not very much use trying to imagine that we are taking part in an Entrance Rite. Sometimes we can detect the appropriateness of the psalm to the feast or to the rest of the Mass for the particular day. Sometimes, on the other hand, the antiphon will not be taken from the psalms but from some other part of Holy Scripture or may even be of ecclesiastical composition. On the whole, if we are to participate in the Introit at all apart from singing it (that is a question which will not engage us until we treat later on of High Mass), it looks as though we should have to fall back on a favourite reflection of pious authors since the 9th century that these Old Testament texts may be looked upon as the cry of the patriarchs awaiting Christ's coming. If we are to maintain in any way the original significance of the Introit, it is obvious that we must not follow the common practice of remaining on our knees while it is being said.

The Entrance Rite in its original form, a procession accompanied by psalmody, was presumably concluded, like all such

---

[1] On the altar and on the eucharistic furniture and ornaments in general I must refer to Canon Crogaert's exhaustive three-volume work, *Les Rites et Prières du Saint Sacrifice de la Messe*, sumptuously illustrated; a shortened English version of it is being prepared.

[2] On certain occasions, for example on Good Friday when the primitive form of the Synaxis is preserved, there is no Introit.

rites, with a collect prayer. But in the 5th or 6th century the *Kyrie Eleison*, and (for certain occasions) the *Gloria* were interposed. The former was a popular acclamation sung by clergy and people alternately. Abbot Cabrol[1] concludes that it is a residuum of the sort of litany which we still use on Holy Saturday and Rogation Days. And it seems that it was borrowed from the Eastern rites, not used primitively at Rome by Greek-speaking Christians. It is addressed directly to Christ, which is contrary to the regular Roman procedure of addressing God the Father through Christ our Lord. Our existing Liturgy has grown up in some respects as the result of historical accidents, but this should not blind us to the advantages which it offers. Here the juxtaposition (in all Masses of a festal character) of the *Kyrie Eleison* and the *Gloria* sets before us again the two themes of supplication and of triumph which we noticed at the beginning.

The *Gloria* is a Christian hymn of great antiquity, possibly one of those referred to by Pliny in the second century. Its magnificent simplicity hardly requires commentary. But it may be well to observe that it falls not into three parts, each addressed to one of the three Persons of the Trinity, but into four. The first part makes no distinction between the Persons; it is only at the words *Deus Pater Omnipotens* that the distinct invocations of the several Persons begin. *Gratias agimus tibi propter magnam gloriam tuam* expresses with peculiar felicity the spirit of the Liturgy, the adoration of God because he is who he is. The Collect which follows (there was never more than one *oratio* at Rome in the early Christian centuries) received its name either because the people were gathered together for the *Synaxis* or because it gathered together into a formal petition the people's litany.[2] In either case it is peculiarly a prayer said in the name of all, presenting to God their needs and their intentions. Naturally it is introduced by the *Dominus Vobiscum*. It should be heard distinctly by the whole congregation and solemnly ratified with the *Amen*. The characteristics of the Roman *Oratio* must be left for more detailed consideration later when we turn to the Propers of the liturgical seasons. But we must note at once the sublimity and simplicity of their

---

[1] *Op. cit.* p. 52.   [2] The first explanation is now the accepted one.

theology. To take an example at random, on the 17th Sunday after Pentecost we pray that we may seek after God alone with a pure mind: *te solum Deum pura mente sectari.* Could anything be closer to the heart of the matter? That is typical.

We have seen that the earliest form of the *Synaxis* began with reading from the Scriptures. The Roman rite had three lessons originally, as the older Masses in the Missal testify, the first being from the Old Testament. Then they were reduced to the two which we have to-day, the Epistle and the Gospel. They were always interspersed with a considerable amount of psalmody, which survives to some extent in the Gradual which follows the Epistle. The Gradual is therefore more ancient than any other variable part of the Mass. It was sung by one or two cantors and was a responsory; that is, the faithful responded by repeating a verse. The complicated Gregorian Graduals, lovely as they are, are thus in a sense regrettable since they militated against the people's participation. The Epistle was read or chanted from an ambo or pulpit on the south side, and the Gradual, when it became the custom for a choir to sing it, from the steps of the ambo, which accounts for its name. The Alleluia is another responsory, originally separated from the Gradual by a Lesson, and now coming directly after it (in Paschal time an extra Alleluia replaces the Gradual). The Tract, which replaces the Alleluia on penitential occasions, was a psalm sung straight through; it is usually much cut down in our Masses, and in some cases it is not taken from the psalms at all. Sequences occur at this point in the modern Roman rite, but so rarely that they must be passed over in so summary an account as this. I have dwelt somewhat on the origins of this part of the *Synaxis,* because it is difficult to make anything of it at Low Mass unless we exert our historical imaginations.

We are now at the point at which the Missal is carried over to the north side for the reading of the Gospel. The Gospel ambo was on the north side, apparently because it was considered more fitting for the deacon to face the men's side. (Anyhow it would have been his natural position—on the President's *right*— in the ancient basilica). As regards Low Mass, one would prefer to see in this practice a convenient arrangement for leaving the south side of the altar clear for preparing the Offertory rather than as a summons to the heathens of the north to hear the Gospel! But the latter explanation has been popular since the 10th century. There is no reason why the congregation should not make use of the prayer said by the priest in the middle of the altar while the book is being carried round, for it is the duty of us all to proclaim the Gospel wherever we have opportunity, and we may well ask for our hearts and lips to be purified that we may undertake so great a task in humility and reverence and with a full sense of our responsibility. It may remind us too of the magnificence of the ancient procession to the Gospel ambo which to-day, even at High Mass, is much shorn of its beauty. For instance, the Gospel book was kissed by all the clergy and, in some places, by the faithful also. We might bear in mind when we sign ourselves with the cross on the forehead, lips and breast that this is the climax of the *Synaxis*. Some writers draw a parallel between the movement of this preparatory rite and that of the Sacrifice itself. In each case we offer to God that we may be worthy to receive from him. Here, after our service of praise and petition, we receive his word.

The sermon ought to explain anything in the Mass of the day which needs explaining, and nowadays it is often very necessary to preach on the fundamental meaning of the Mass. Here I cannot resist repeating an opinion recently expressed by Fr Clifford Howell, S.J., although its bearing on our immediate concern is somewhat indirect. Let the instruction be given at the *last* Mass, Fr Howell urged, because the people who attend that Mass need it more; and let it be a Low Mass, if by that arrangement you can have a sung Mass earlier at which the more zealous parishioners communicate—they can do without a sermon if necessary. But I must not pursue the subject of the Sung Mass at present. I would only add in connection with the sermon that if we do not come across the sort of sermon we want it is easily supplied not only by the abundant liturgical literature of our own day but by the Patristic sermons, which are now accessible in English in the series published by the (American) Newman Press and in French in the series *Sources Chrétiennes*. It is of the highest importance that the educated laity should have some acquaintance with the sermons of, say, St Augustine and St Leo, which are often suited so perfectly to the needs of modern readers.

The *Synaxis* is now at an end, but before the Offertory there is
the Creed on Sundays and the greater feastdays, including their
octaves. All that need be said about it here is that it uses the
singular form because creeds were formulae said by each of the
candidates for Baptism and thus it is eminently suitable that
we should all make our professions of faith at this point—
the server (in England, at least) is supposed to kneel, but it is
surely undesirable for the congregation to do so.

It is also undesirable in itself for the congregation to sit down
when the priest begins the Offertory rite with a *Dominus
Vobiscum* (as if he had turned to the people and said "You can
take it easy for the present"—that is the impression so often
actually produced). It is true that after the *Oremus* no prayer
follows, only the Offertory antiphon, and it may be that the
Dominus Vobiscum looks ahead to the secret prayer at the end
of the Offertory or is a mere survival of intercessory prayers
which were said before the beginning of the Sacrifice (as still
to-day on Good Fridays at the end of the *Synaxis*). But it ought
to be in effect a call to immediate prayer on any showing, for the
Offertory itself is the liturgical act of the whole congregation,
priest and people; it begins what they have come together to *do*.
By themselves bringing the gifts of bread and wine for the
Eucharist, the faithful used to make it clear in the Offertory
procession, which seems to appear in the 4th century, that the
Sacrifice is the Sacrifice of the Church in the sense of the famous
passage in St Augustine's *De Civitate Dei*, chapter 20: "the
sacrifice which we offer every day is the Sacrifice of the Church,
which being the body of Christ, who is its head, learns through
him to sacrifice herself". He had previously told us in an
equally famous passage from the sixth chapter that "the whole
city of the redeemed, that is the assembly of the faithful, which
is the universal sacrifice, is offered to God by the High Priest,
who offered himself for us in his Passion". We have, then, an
essential part to play in the drama of our transformation into
Christ. By thus presenting ourselves to him we make it possible
for the work of the Redemption to be exercised—*opus nostrae
Redemptionis exercetur*, to use once more the often-quoted
secret prayer for the 9th Sunday after Pentecost. The fruits of
the Mass, we have to remember, are not just automatically

produced. It rests with us to see to it that they are abundant. The partial revival of the Offertory procession in our day is one of the clearest signs that we are regaining a real understanding of the Liturgy.

The Offertory chant, like those of the Introit and the Communion, was originally a processional psalm of which only a fragment remains in our present rite. Its antiphon, like the other antiphons, has lost touch (as a rule) with its original purpose. It was sung by a choir and may have been concluded, like the other chants, with a formal prayer. Just as the *Kyrie Eleison* and the *Gloria* were inserted between the Introit and the Collect, so the silent Offertory prayers which the priest says to-day were inserted in mediaeval times between the Offertory chant and the Secret prayers. As before, we must be on our guard here against any tendency to under-value them on that account. They are developed forms of prayers which had been in use for centuries, and they contain some highly significant and impressive phrases. The first, *Suscipe, sancte Pater*, said while the host is offered on the raised paten, is the priest's offering of his own gift. But, since we are all supposed to be making one in our hearts, it is most suitable that we should make use of it ourselves. The phrase *hanc hostiam immaculatam* looks forward to the Consecration and emphasizes, as do so many of the Secret prayers, that we offer our gifts precisely that they may become Christ's Body and Blood. The prayer ends by referring to the *intentions* of the congregation and of the whole Christian Church. The priest offers in the name of the congregation, but it would be the most disastrous misunderstanding to suppose that the faithful do not therefore offer themselves, a misunderstanding for which there is no excuse since the truth is so plain to see in the whole history of the Mass and in the very text of the Roman Rite, as we shall have occasion to observe.

The symbolism of the mixing of water and wine has already been touched upon. It is the chief reason for the occurrence at this point of the glorious prayer *Deus qui humanae substantiae*, which the faithful should certainly be encouraged to use. It is an old Roman Christmas Collect with a reference added to the wine and the water, and it sums up the Christian mystery in an inimitable way: through Christ's humanity we are to be made partakers of his divinity. The prayer *Offerimus* follows. The plural form of the prayer has reference to the help which the priest received from the deacon in raising the large chalices used in early times (the deacon still touches the foot of the chalice at High Mass). The phrase contained in it, "for the salvation of the whole world", should be echoing in our minds throughout the Sacrifice. The next prayer, asking that we may be received by God in the spirit of humility and with a contrite heart, makes it perfectly clear that our gifts, which are to become Christ's Body and Blood, stand for ourselves. Thus, the prayer continues, the Sacrifice will be acceptable. It quotes from the prayer of the three young men in the fiery furnace, a passage from the book of Daniel which puts before us in a very striking way the dispositions which God requires for sacrifice. Then comes the invocation of the Holy Spirit, *Veni Sanctificator*. The transubstantiating of our gifts is attributed especially to God the Holy Spirit, like the Incarnation itself and the bestowal of all supernatural gifts upon the Church. And it is noteworthy that we pray for the *Sacrifice* to be *blessed*; the meaning which the Liturgy gives to sacrifice is therefore plain enough.

The priest now washes the tips of his fingers. The meaning of this was and is symbolic, although it came to have a practical utility as well. The appropriateness of the *Lavabo* psalm at this point has been brought out verse by verse by the devotion of commentators, but it hardly needs comment. There is still one more prayer before the *Orate Fratres*: the *Suscipe, Sancta Trinitas*. It is a doublet of the previous prayer *In spiritu humilitatis*, and its commemoration of Christ's passion, resurrection and ascension and its invocation of the saints are anticipations of the Canon. We may therefore pass on, with the reminder that all these prayers are adaptable for the laity's use.

The *Orate Fratres* with its reference to "my sacrifice and yours" has been often quoted of late years to demonstrate—unnecessarily—the laity's share in the sacrifice. Unfortunately the rubric prescribes that only the first two words of it should be said aloud and these only "in a slightly raised voice", thus preserving contact with the original practice of addressing the assistant ministers (*fratres*) at this time. A general summons to prayer would be eminently suitable here, for the Secret prayer formally sums up the Offertory. As Pierre le Brun remarks, "nearly all the Secret prayers amount to the request *that God will favourably receive the gifts which are on the altar and by his grace make us fit to be ourselves presented to him as an acceptable offering*".[1] "The priest raises his voice", Pierre le Brun continues, "at the *per omnia saecula saeculorum* at the end of the prayer. In the prayer which he has said in secret the fire of divine love should have been lighted in his heart, and as if he were emerging from an ecstacy, eager to secure the collaboration of all the assistants in the prayer which he has just said, he breaks silence and invites the whole assembly to join him and to reply 'Amen'. This reply has always been made with enthusiasm, and St Jerome tells us that it echoed through the churches like a thunderclap. The faithful thus give their approval to all that the priest has asked for from God in secret, and they must be well persuaded, says Theodoret, that in answering 'Amen' they share in all the prayers which the priest has been saying alone."[2] That is the way in which an 18th century writer looked at the Secret. The practice of saying the "prayer over the oblations" secretly came to Rome from the north in about the 8th century—the same custom was introduced for the Canon in the same way a little later. Two examples of Secret prayers may now suffice: *Munus quod tibi, Domine, nostrae servitutis offerimus Tu salutare nobis perfice sacramentum* (Monday after the 3rd Sunday in Lent) "this offering which our devotion makes to you, Lord, make for us the sacrament of our salvation". Again, rather longwindedly for a Secret, but with magnificent completeness: *Domine Deus noster qui in his potius creaturis, quas ad fragilitatis nostrae subsidium contulisti, tuo quoque nomini munera jussisti dicanda constitui: tribue, quaesumus, ut et vitae nobis praesentis auxilium et aeternitatis efficiant sacramentum* (Thursday after Passion Sunday) "Lord, our God, you who have chosen these creatures made by you and bidden us consecrate them to your name as offerings, grant, we pray, that they may be both the support of our present life and the sacrament of life everlasting".

[1] This is the point at which to note that the Offertory is, historically, an outgrowth from the Canon, and must be understood in terms of the Canon.

[2] *Op. cit.* p. 345. (In fact St Jerome refers to the "Amen" of the Canon.)

V

THE ORDINARY OF THE MASS:
THE CANON

IN 1949 A BOOK APPEARED BY DOM JEROME GASSNER, A MONK of Seitenstetten, *The Canon of the Mass, its History, Theology and Art*.[1] I am bound to say that it is not an easy book to read, but it contains a great deal of most valuable matter, and the passage which I shall now quote seems to be precisely the introduction which we need to our present subject: "The name and the present function of the preface do not reveal that it is itself the most ancient element of the Canon, that together with the final doxology it constitutes the original Eucharistic prayer. Although externally reduced to an introduction of the Canon, it has preserved all fundamental ideas and is ideologically so intimately connected with the present Canon that what is now called the Canon has to be explained as the result of the organic unfolding of the ideas proclaimed in the few words of the preface.

"The original Canon is the most jubilant hymn of thanksgiving, the most triumphant chant of the glory of God. This Eucharistic canticle *katexochen*, this first song of Christendom, is most sacred in origin and character, most sublime in its ideology, most comprehensive in significance and efficacy. It has incorporated on the one hand the great hymn inspired by the Holy Ghost: the canticle of Moses, the first hymn contained in divine revelation; the Hallel of the Old Testament, the most solemn hymn of the liturgy of the Temple. The original Canon is the continuation of the hymn of the Last Supper, a paraphrase of our Lord's prayer of thanksgiving before the institution of the mysteries of His body and blood. That prayer forms the most sacred nucleus of the Canon. It resounds finally in the melodies of the canticle of the heavenly liturgy, revealed in the Apocalypse. The original Canon is, on the other hand,

[1] Published in America by Herder.

the model and exemplar for the rest of the most venerable hymns of the liturgy, of Christian antiquity: it has inspired the symbols of faith, the *Gloria in excelsis*, the *Exultet*, the *Te Deum*."[1] "The canticle of Moses and the Hallel" (Psalms cxii.-cxiii. and cxxxv), Dom Gassner remarks later[2] "are equally triumphant, victorious, Eucharistic hymns, both foreshadow the victory of Christ over sin and the devil, his glorious entry into heaven, the victory of his Saints, and their triumphant entrance into the heavenly paradise." The liturgy of the Apocalypse, which is so closely connected with the Hallel, we shall find referred to in the emphasis laid upon the angelic worship in the Eucharistic prayer and in the twenty-four saints of the prayer *Communicantes* corresponding with the twenty-four ancients before the throne of God. In the great sacerdotal prayer of St John's seventeenth chapter, Dom Gassner explains, our Lord's formal consecration of himself is introduced by a prayer in two parts for his own glorification and ended by a prayer in two parts for the glorification of his disciples and their followers. It seems that the Canon of the Mass echoes this arrangement with the prayer *Te Igitur* and its continuation *Quam Oblationem* before the Consecration, and with the *Communicantes* and the *Nobis quoque peccatoribus* after it. The coincidence of the theme of *unity* is especially remarkable in the passage from St John and in the Canon, which clearly takes over from that passage our Lord's raising his eyes to heaven and his tender addresses to his heavenly Father.[3] The influence of St Paul, though considerable, is less pervasive.

We may also accept from Dom Gassner his descriptions of the Canon as a mosaic and as a dramatic poem. Thus we might apply to it the notion of "dramatic time" and explain that some of the invocations which precede the Consecration and which are at first sight puzzling in this position are anticipatory. The Canon, Dom Gassner tells us, influenced and was influenced by the great mosaics of Rome and Ravenna. So in San Vitale we have the sacrifices of Abel, Abraham, Melchisedech and the Lamb of God borne up by four angels. There is the same hieratic style, the same symmetrical symbolism, the same decomposing and radiating of light outwards from the centre in

---

[1] pp. 53-4.   [2] p. 56.   [3] Gassner, *op. cit.* pp. 22-5.

the mosaics and in the Canon. Its richness of content is indicated by the profusion of names used of it; to quote only some
of them, it is called the theology, the action, the *agenda*, the
proclamation (*praedicatio*), the profession (*contestatio*), the
immolation, the offering (*anaphora*), the mystery or simply the
prayer (*prex*).

But we must not allow enthusiasm to make us undiscriminating. We may indeed discover a fittingness in all the parts of
the existing Canon. But we must admit a certain loss of clarity
and unity when we compare it with the preface and anaphora
ascribed by Dom Hugh Connolly to St Hippolytus and belonging to the first part of the 3rd century:

> We render thanks to Thee, O God, through Thy well-beloved
> Son Jesus Christ, that in these last days Thou has sent Him as
> Saviour and Redeemer and Angel (messenger) of Thy Will,
> Who is Thine inseparable Word, by Whom Thou hast made
> all things, and in Whom Thou art well pleased. Thou hast
> sent Him from heaven into the Virgin's womb, where He
> became incarnate and manifested Himself as Thy Son, born
> of the Holy Ghost and the Virgin; then accomplishing Thy
> Will and conquering a new and holy race, He stretched out
> His Hands in His Passion in order that He might deliver from
> suffering those who have believed in Thee: and at the moment
> when He delivered Himself voluntarily to his Passion, in
> order to destroy death, to break the devil's chains, to spurn
> hell under His feet, to enlighten the just, to fix a term, to show
> forth the Resurrection, taking the Bread and giving thanks,
> He said: "Take, eat: This is My Body which shall be broken
> for you." Likewise the cup, saying: "This is My Blood
> which is shed for you: when you do this, you do it in memory
> of Me."
>
> Remembering, then, His Death and Resurrection, we offer
> Thee this Bread and this Chalice, thanking Thee because Thou
> hast deigned to permit us to appear before Thee and to serve
> Thee. And we pray Thee to send Thy Holy Spirit upon the
> oblation of the Holy Church, and uniting them as one, that
> Thou wilt give to all the Saints who participate [in the
> Sacrifice] to be filled with the Holy Ghost and fortified in the

truth of the Faith, so that we may praise Thee and glorify Thee by Thy Child Jesus Christ, by Whom to Thee is glory and honour, to the Father, Son, and Holy Ghost, in Your Holy Church, now and for all ages. Amen.

This shows us plainly how the thanksgiving prayer or offering (the two ideas are inextricably blended) develops into a consecratory narrative which is at the same time an *anamnesis* or commemoration of the historical Christian mystery and an identifying of the offering with that mystery. That this identification is consummated in Holy Communion is brought out by the earliest witness of all to the details of the Roman Mass. St Justin, writing in the 2nd century, tells us that bread and wine mingled with water are brought to the President of the assembly, who recites a prayer over them, after which they are distributed to the faithful by the deacons. "For we take not that food", he writes, "as common bread and common drink. Just as, by virtue of the Word of God, Jesus Christ Our Saviour took flesh and blood for our salvation, thus the Food consecrated by the prayer formed of the very words of Christ Himself, that Food which nourishes by assimilation our own body and blood, is the Flesh and Blood of Jesus Incarnate. Such is our doctrine."

It is tempting to pursue the subject of the Roman Mass in ancient times, to quote for example Père Bouyer's moving description[1] of the *Synaxis* in a Roman Basilica, with the people grouped round the ministers and the altar, that is round Christ the high priest and Christ the victim, with the whole assembly surrounded by the dignified magnificence of early Christian art, which portrayed the whole creation waiting before the empty throne. "Maranatha! Come, Lord Jesus." It is tempting, too, to pursue another theme of Dom Gassner's, that of the Canon as a mosaic, in particular, of Scriptural texts; few enquiries are more illuminating and rewarding. But the limits of our undertaking oblige us to select only a few details from each of the divisions into which the prayer falls, and we must turn to them at once.

The extreme solemnity of the opening dialogue makes it clear that the action itself is now beginning. We must not think

[1] In *Le Mystère Pascal*.

of it as a mere prelude despite its exclusion from the Canon in our modern Missals. The "Preface", as we now call it, advances regularly (that for the Apostles is a notable exception) to the proclamation of the divine titles, addressing in majestic terms the God to whom thanks are offered; it then invokes the mediation of Christ or enunciates the particular reason for thanksgiving, the particular aspect of the Christian mystery, which is proper to the feast or the season, and concludes by associating us with the angelic worship, the Benedictus, as St Thomas says,[1] emphasizing that this worship is due to the *Incarnate* Word, to Christ as both God and man. (Dom Gassner points out that the heavenly high-priesthood of Christ is referred to in the phrase *per Christum Dominum* no less than seven times during the Canon, thrice before the Consecration and four times after it.) At this point we must allow ourselves a reference to the corresponding formulae of the Byzantine liturgy: "We who mystically represent the cherubim and join with them in singing the thrice holy hymn to the lifegiving Trinity, let us lay aside all the cares of this life ... for we are now to receive the King of all, who comes escorted by unseen hosts of angels, Alleluja, alleluja, alleluja ... We give thanks also for that Thou art pleased to accept this service from our hands, while there stand about Thee legions of archangels and myriads of angels and cherubim and seraphim, six-winged and many-eyed, who, borne aloft upon their wings, sing, cry out, and shout the triumphal song, saying: Holy, Holy, Holy."

The singing of the *Sanctus* may not be as primitive as the opening dialogue between priest and people; but it seems to have been in liturgical use in Apostolic times; in some places at least this acclamation also was sung by the people to the simple tune used by the priest for the Preface. The most profound significance of the liturgical *Sanctus* is that it is the fulfilment and explanation of the great theophanies of the Old Testament, the revelation of the Exodus, the visions of Isaias, Ezechiel and Daniel, all of them gathered up in the vision of the Apocalypse (which indeed may be rather the effect than the cause of the Eucharistic hymn) and that it is "the sacramental anticipation of the beatific vision".[2] The theme of Christ's headship over the

[1] *Summa Theol.* III a, q. 83.   [2] Gassner, *op. cit.* p. 143 (cf. the whole chapter).

angels shows the influence of St Paul. "For the Eucharist", says P. Bouyer, "is the recapitulation of the whole creation in Christ of which St Paul has given us the general notion and which St Irenaeus has profoundly developed. In the Eucharist, humanity and the material world which depends on it, after falling away from God, running counter to the divine plan through the revolt of Satan and his angels, returns to it by Christ. Hence the cosmic bearing of the eucharistic prayer."[1] The Eastern Liturgies here recall the whole divine economy up to the evening of Maundy Thursday: the Roman Preface sums up the scope of the thanksgiving at the beginning in the two words *semper* and *ubique*. And so at the end of the Preface we rejoin those angelic hosts who have never fallen, who have never ceased to sing the *Sanctus*, for we are now, like them, true created images of the uncreated Image, mirroring the Son's eternal "eucharist" in the bosom of the Father. Heaven and earth are now full of God's glory, for the coming of the Son of David is his manifestation. *Hosanna in excelsis. Benedictus qui venit in nomine Domini. Hosanna in excelsis.* "These acclamations", writes Dom Gassner, "apply historically to the nativity of the Messiah, to his entry for His sacrifice in Jerusalem, to His second coming. These significations are implied also in the Benedictus of the Canon: it means the re-enactment of the Nativity, His entry to the sacrifice, the anticipation of His glorious coming."[2]

The eucharistic anaphora of St Hippolytus, who claims that it is of apostolic origin, passed, as we have seen, straight from our Preface to the consecratory narrative *Qui pridie.* ... Of the five prayers which have intervened, the first, the *Te igitur*, was probably added, although not quite in its present form,[3] by the end of the 4th century, together with some form of the last (the *Quam oblationem*), the fourth (the *Hanc Oblationem*) being added not much later. The insertion of the rest may be assigned to the 7th century (these dates, here as elsewhere, are those which appear to be generally accepted by liturgists). What was the intention of the Church in making these additions? The

---

[1] *Le Mystère Pascal*, cf. chap. III §3 for this and for what immediately follows.
[2] *Op. cit.* p. 169. "Re-enactment" however, as I have suggested in chap. III, is a misleading word.
[3] This restriction must often be understood to apply to formulae described as "primitive".

Te igitur clearly continues the Preface, picking it up, as it were, at the point at which the solemn address to God takes place; it asks that our offering should be accepted, making it explicit that the thanksgiving of the Preface is itself an offering, *which offering*, the Canon goes on to say a little later, is to become precisely Christ's own offering, himself. The intervening prayer (*Hanc oblationem*) is, according to Baumstark's interpretation (which seems altogether reasonable), a later expansion, including an intercessory prayer originally variable for particular occasions but now fixed for the general intentions of the offerers at all times. The introduction into the Canon of this theme of explicit intercession obviously accounts also for the presence of the last part of the *Te igitur*, for the *Memento* of the living and for the remaining prayer, the *Communicantes*. Finally, in this general survey of the pre-consecratory prayers, we may notice that the *Hanc oblationem* introduces as well the explicit theme of propitiation. The rubric that the priest holds his hands outspread over the offerings at that point expresses this.

We may now note a few points of detail. Dom Gassner[1] tells us that we shall understand better the development of this part of the Canon if we observe that in the narrative of institution the phrase "giving thanks, he blessed" is employed. The oldest form of the Canon speaks only of "giving thanks". The addition of the word "blessed" in the Roman Canon is accompanied by the addition of the pre-consecratory invocations. "The thanksgiving prayer of the ancient anaphora", Dom Gassner writes, "is one continuous phrase, whereby the 'thanksgiving' of the priest is identified with the thanksgiving of Christ [at the Last Supper]."[2] In our rite the *Qui pridie* joins the two thanksgivings, and thus the Preface itself still contains the petition for transubstantiation *per Christum Dominum*. "Giving thanks" and "blessing" are synonymous expressions in the New Testament. The accounts of the Last Supper use either the one or the other but never both. The Church, Dom Gassner thinks, in her anxiety to preserve the full force of the words of Scripture, has brought out the meaning more fully by employing both these expressions, and the thanksgiving which is also a blessing and

[1] Chaps. XV and XVI.   [2] pp. 188-9.

the blessing which is also a thanksgiving thus receive separate treatment. So *igitur* at the beginning of our Canon connects the thanksgiving of the Preface with the invocations which follow. And thus there are correspondences to be found between these two parts of our eucharistic prayer: *supplices* in the *Te igitur* for example corresponds with the *supplici confessione* of the Preface.

There are also correspondences to be found within the pre-consecratory invocations themselves, such as the uses of the superlative at the beginning of the first and at the end of the last (*clementissime Pater ... dilectissimi Filii tui*). But we must confine ourselves now to considering only a few features in these prayers which seem to require particular explanation. The reference in the first prayer to the "unspotted host" may be proleptic. The *cultoribus* at the end of it are not the "worshippers" in general (although often translated as such), but the "tillers" of the Lord's vineyard—bishops and, probably, promoters of the faith such as founders of churches. The following prayer, *Memento*, refers first to benefactors or others specially prayed for, then to the congregation as a whole; "for whom we offer or who themselves offer", the text reads—that is to say, whether they are present or not. When the people ceased to bring up bread and wine the priest in fact always offered *for them*, but the prayer originally envisaged the Offertory procession. The word *Communicantes* at the beginning of the next prayer has given rise to a great deal of discussion, but the obvious solution would seem to be that it is simply a continuation of the *Memento*, the present participle agreeing with the subject in *reddunt* just above, that is, the offerers. The saints mentioned in this prayer were finally arranged by Pope St Gregory I, by whom the last touches to the Canon were made (it does not seem that he was responsible for any far-reaching changes). Twelve apostles are balanced by twelve martyrs to make up the number of the ancients of the Apocalypse. The first five martyrs are Popes (Linus and Cletus being added to fill in the list between St Peter and St Clement); the remainder were venerated in Rome (for reasons of varying cogency) at the time. We have seen that the phrase *per eumdem Christum Dominum* at the end of the prayer is altogether apposite and need not be regarded as breaking up the Canon. But the same cannot be said of the *Amen* (which also occurs at the end of the *Hanc igitur*). There is room for only one *Amen* in the Canon—at the end.

"The Canon", writes Dom Gassner, in an inelegant but effective paragraph, "is a preparation for the words of consecration, a mirror, an extension of them. The Canon is the theology of the Holy Eucharist, of the power and the effect of the divine words. Under the guidance of the Holy Ghost, the Church has surrounded these divine words with a fragrant wreath, with a glorious halo, whereby nature and grace, art and faith, vie with one another in the effort to express the great hidden truth."[1] As regards the Roman formulae of consecration we must be content to notice that words have been supplied from what seem to have been Petrine formulas as well as from St Paul to build up both a complete account and an exact parallelism, and that very striking Old Testament types of our Lord's words are to be found in the words of Moses about the Pasch. Finally, as regards the ceremonial of the Consecration, it is generally known that the elevation of the Host and the ringing of bells were not introduced until the early middle ages, but less generally that this led to the practice of genuflecting before the Blessed Sacrament, which was not adopted in the Roman rite until the 14th century: it has no place in the Eastern Liturgy.

Here, at the supreme moment of the Mass, we must again accept P. Bouyer's guidance. Our bread and wine become Christ's body and blood, and by this means we are associated with his sacrifice. That, says P. Bouyer, is one way of looking at it, but there is another: it is because Christ has given us his own act of offering to perform that he has identified himself with our food and drink. "Thus we become by the Mass what he became by the Cross: a living oblation to God his Father". This leads us to the conclusion that his enabling of us to give ourselves to his love is his redemptive gift *par excellence*.[2]

In considering the prayers which follow the Consecration it will be convenient to treat first the primitive elements, the *anamnesis* and the final doxology, leaving until later the intercessory prayers which were interpolated later very much in the

[1] p. 247.   [2] *Loc. cit.*

same way as the pre-consecratory invocations. The *anamnesis* (*unde et memores*) takes up the last words of the consecration-narrative and develops them. It declares that what we offer *is* now the Christian mystery, the various phases of which are naturally commemorated. *Offerimus* refers to the whole congregation. As in the *Te igitur* we find references to the spotlessness of the Sacrifice emphasized by signs of the cross. The doxology *Per Ipsum* ... is the triumphal conclusion of the Canon, and the Host and Chalice used to be raised to some height above the *mensa*, not to be seen by the people, but as a gesture of offering. The "Little Elevation", as it is now called, must not be thought of as a ceremony of secondary importance; there is no more significant gesture in the Liturgy. The grandeur of the language, *per ipsum et cum ipso et in ipso*, is enough in itself to show us this. It seems a pity that the words *per omnia saecula saeculorum* now follow the elevation instead of accompanying it as they did until the 15th century. The ratifying of the whole Canon by the people's *Amen* has been insisted upon at all times to the degree in which the mystery of our faith has been appreciated. Nothing could be more unseemly than for the priest to supply this himself after vainly expecting a mumble of acquiescence from a server.

Turning back to the prayers which follow the *anamnesis*, we may first note that they have the same function as the *Te igitur* group of making explicit the character of our petitions. The first two, *Supra quae* and *Supplices*, are the most venerable, having been established in this place since the 4th century. In the first we ask God, now that he has placed the Sacrifice of his Son beneath the sign of ours, to accept this Sacrifice of the whole Mystical Body, even as he accepted those sacrifices which were only its foreshadowing, the first sacrifice of all, that of Abel (the reference to it in the Epistle to the Hebrews is in mind), the sacrificial gesture of Abraham which sealed the Old Alliance, the sacrifice of Melchisedech which was a prophetic promise of the New. In the second of these prayers, the *Supplices*, we return to the theme of the angelic worship with the special purpose of pleading that the earthly altar may be *effectively* united with the heavenly, that through the acceptance of our Sacrifice we may be fruitfully united with God in Holy

Communion. "The Communion", says the Encyclical *Mediator*, "belongs to the integration of the Sacrifice". "No sacrament", writes P. Bouyer, "can have a magical effect so as to transform us, as it were, from outside, since our inward transformation on the contrary is the purpose of them all. The great sacrament of reconciliation, then, puts at our disposal what Christ has done, so that his act may become ours. But this coincidence will be an intimate one only in so far as we accept it and beg that it may become such. That is the meaning of the prayer *Supplices* ... corresponding to the *epiclesis* of the Eastern Liturgies which pray at this point for the descent of the Holy Spirit upon the holy gifts. There is no further need for them to be objectively sanctified—this has been done already by Christ's word, which has itself sanctified them—but the Holy Spirit must still sanctify their subjective reception by ourselves."[1] But it must be recognized that some authors see in this latter part of the Canon the traces of a retrospective prayer for consecration.

The remaining prayers, *Memento*, *Nobis quoque peccatoribus* and *Per Quem* became generally established in the 6th and 7th centuries. The first two balance the earlier *Memento* prayer and the *Communicantes*. The thought of communion is still to the fore in these intercessory prayers. The "sign of faith" in the *Memento* refers to the baptismal rite, and we see in this prayer the language of early Christian epigraphy. The *Amen* at the end of it we may be permitted to regret, as also that at the end of the *Supplices*, just above. The *Nobis quoque peccatoribus* carries on the thought of the *Supplices* (referring not only to the ministers, but to the whole assembly[2]) by introducing the theme of eternal life, which led later to the list of saints which follow. The names in this prayer were arranged, like those of the prayer *Communicantes*, by Pope Gregory I. After St John (the Baptist) the names of fourteen martyrs follow, seven men and seven women. Felicity is the Roman martyr, not Perpetua's slave of that name, who would be mentioned after her, not before. Information about the other martyrs, so far as there is any, is sufficiently accessible. There remains the prayer *Per Quem haec omnia*, the interpretation of which has been the subject of some dispute. Here it seems best to borrow another

---

[1] *Loc. cit.*   [2] Although not *clara voce* (*La Maison Dieu*, 23, p. 44).

paragraph from Fr Coventry: "The formula, *Per Quem*, we know to have been in use for the blessing of various objects such as milk, honey, etc. and the Bishop still blesses the oils at this place on Maundy Thursday. The custom of introducing such a blessing-formula into the Canon was due to people wanting to have the blessings linked as closely as possible with the Blessing, the Eucharistic Prayer. We have already noted that many other gifts apart from those of bread and wine were brought up in the Offertory procession, and these would be placed beside the altar; well into the Middle Ages many natural objects were blessed at this point, apart from those given to the Church. This fact accounts for the wording of the prayer which does not primarily refer to the Bread and the Wine now already consecrated, though these are included as may be seen from the last phrase, *praestas nobis* ('dost give to us'), which has the coming Communion in mind. The prayer is not a petition for a blessing, but a recognition and appreciation of the great Blessing, the Consecration, that has already taken place."

The Communion rite will be dealt with very briefly by way of appendix. I shall not stop to describe the affecting simplicity and splendour of the ancient form of administration or to dwell on the words of the Eastern Liturgies, which speak, for example, of the burning coal, the *anthrax*, and the cup of fire. The *Pater Noster*, then, was placed next after the Canon by St Gregory the Great in conformity with the Eastern practice. Its solemn introduction is a reminder of the time when it was a closely guarded secret. The *Amen* at the end of it is again an intrusive one, since the prayer *Libera nos* is really a continuation. At this point occurred the "breaking of bread" which gave to the Mass the first of all its titles. In the days of unleavened bread it was a lengthy business. The breaking of the Host, which occurs at the end of the *Libera nos* in our Roman rite, is a relic of the practice whereby the Pope or the Bishop would send portions of the Host consecrated by him to other priests in the neighbourhood, who would place them in their own chalices as a sign of the *unity* of the Eucharist in all places. The placing of a small piece of the Host in the chalice (broken off from one of the divided halves) seems to derive from the custom of dipping a piece of the

Host in the unconsecrated wine given to the faithful after their
Communion. The various symbolic interpretations which have
been placed on these rites need not detain us. In practice we
may regard them as signs of the unity of the faithful with Christ
and with one another, connected as they are by the *Pax
Domini*, the primitive Kiss of Peace. The theme of peace is added
to that of unity in the prayers which follow. The *Agnus Dei*,
originally introduced in the 7th century as an acclamation by the
people during the breaking, was later associated with the *Pax*.
The rest of the Communion prayers down to the Communion
chant are medieval compositions which did not become
established here until the 16th century, as is shown (for example)
by the use of the first person. But they are to be treated as poor
relations no more than the somewhat similar Offertory prayers.
To the Communion chant and the Post-Communion prayer the
remarks previously made about the Offertory chant and the
Secret are almost precisely applicable. The dates for their
appearances more or less correspond. The Communion procession, like that of the Offertory, was originally accompanied by
a psalm sung by the people, which is now, again as in the case
of the Offertory, reduced to an antiphon. And here again we
may welcome a most encouraging revival of the ancient practice
in our own day. The Post-Communion prayer sums up in the
manner of the Secret, using the same terse and luminous language, the significance of the great act which has been performed. The *Ite missa est* accompanied by a blessing was an
effective dismissal from the 4th century to the 16th, so we may
be entitled here, perhaps, to regard the Ordinary of the Mass as
concluded.

VI

THE LITURGICAL YEAR: I: THE CHRISTMAS CYCLE

IN BEGINNING THE SUBJECT OF THE LITURGICAL YEAR I SHOULD like to draw your attention to a book published by Herder in 1937, *The Year of our Lord*, the English translation of a work by Dame Emiliana Loehr of the Holy Cross Convent, Herstelle. The existence of this translation seems not to be generally known, since the other day there was a notice in the Catholic Press of the appearance of a French translation, and the writer expressed the hope that this would lead to a greater acquaintance with the work of Dame Emiliana among English people who read French but not German. The great advantage of the book is that it contains a liturgical and theological meditation upon the Mass of each Sunday in the year; I do not know of any other single volume in English which has achieved this result. By "a liturgical and theological meditation" I mean a meditation which examines the text of the particular Mass with regard to the fundamental lessons which it teaches us in the context of the liturgical year. Cardinal Schuster's monumental work *The Sacramentary*, and Dom Pius Parsch's deservedly popular guide to the liturgical year are in several volumes. So is Dr Messenger's valuable commentary *The Apostolate of the Sunday Mass*. Abbot Cabrol's book, called in the English translation *The Year's Liturgy*, deals with the Sunday Masses in the first of its two volumes, but its approach is rather historical than theological (I hope I shall not be taken as depreciating the value of this historical approach). Dame Emiliana, on the other hand, bases her work on the doctrine of Dom Odo Casel, and is concerned first and foremost with the particular aspect of the Christian Mystery which the Mass in question puts before us, and with historical questions only in so far as they throw light upon the immediate practical significance of the texts. (I have adopted and shall continue to adopt that method.) A natural result of Dame Emiliana's treatment is that as the book proceeds it tends to produce very much the same considerations over and over again. This is not necessarily a disadvantage, but it has the effect of making the first part of the work by far the most interesting, and I shall confine my references largely to this introductory matter.

But before we turn to the Advent Masses it will be worth our while to select some points of special value for our purposes from the Introductions to Dame Emiliana's book. In addition to her own, there are Introductions by Abbot Vonier and by Dom Casel. Abbot Vonier's is concerned with the way in which past, present and future are brought together in the Liturgy. The past, he points out, is not just a memory for us in the Liturgy. It is an *effective* past, a past which is reproduced for us, operating upon us, because it is contained in the living Christ. At Christmas, for example, Abbot Vonier tells us, it is Christ himself rather than just his historical birth which we celebrate; or we may put it like this: that we have intercourse with him about his birth, his death, his resurrection. Through his intimacy with Christ, the Christian is saved from that isolating of the present from the past and from the future which makes the passing of time for so many men of to-day a mere linear movement, a mere transition from meaningless point to meaningless point. The Christian present is essentially the state of things obtaining between Christ's first and second comings. The Church's life moves between these two poles, is characterized by the influences which each exerts upon it. It both draws continually upon the past and is attracted continually towards the future. For grace is the anticipation of glory. By anticipation, then, the Church shares in some sort in the perpetuity of Christ's existence. And since it is through this perpetuity of Christ, through his risen life, that our personal redemption is conveyed to us, the Resurrection, constituting him in that state of perpetuity, is the supreme fact around which the Church's life revolves.

Dom Casel's essay plunges us at once into a rich system of imagery. It begins by considering the concrete image of the dedicated virgin's ring of espousal, and moves from this to the conception of the holy circle of the mystic liturgical year. This mystic year is an image of that prototype cycle with which

Christ espoused the Church his Bride, that is to say, his cycle of going out from the Father and returning to him again in which we find our Redemption. But to enter into our Redemption we must enter into the mysteries of faith by our liturgical acts, enter into Christ's death and so into his life. The liturgical year has both the movement and the completeness of an *orb*, a revolving circle; it is an activity which is also rest in the Lord. The natural man lives by the course of nature, in an ordered recurring rhythm (and this is a great good when contrasted with the in-human monotony which is the lot of industrialized man): but for the Christian the natural course of the year is only a symbol of that ring with which Christ has wedded our humanity, the ring of the Christian mystery. Dom Casel then develops a favourite theme of his: that the *mysterium* becomes present and effective primarily in the Mass and the sacraments but also in the *sacramentals*—it is present in these various ways in mea-sured proportions; the effect of the sacramentals is not so profound as that of the sacraments, yet we must not unduly confine the Church's life. It is conveyed to us in all that is offered to us by the Church. The Divine Office, then, is a power-ful instrument of our sanctification. In this, too, we find Christ and join him in his continuing redemptive act.

In discussing the origins of the ecclesiastical year, Dom Casel reminds us that originally there was simply the weekly cycle in which each Sunday was a renewal of Easter, the one great Day. Then, he says, the Epiphany was added as the second great feast of the Church's year, and to this, as to Easter, a prepara-tory season was attached. Abbot Cabrol, who approaches the question from the point of view of a Roman liturgist, begins in much the same way by explaining to us that there were origin-ally no Christian feasts except Easter and Pentecost, adding that this was insisted upon by the first generation of Christians who contrasted themselves in that respect with their pagan con-temporaries. Apart from the Wednesday and Friday *Synaxes* the Sunday was the only day of liturgical observance. According to Abbot Cabrol, it was not until devotion to the Holy Places began to develop after the conversion of Constantine that the ecclesiastical year began to be a following of the events of Christ's earthly life. And in Rome it was the feast of Christmas, to which the preparatory season of Advent was later added, which was the beginning of the year;[1] the Epiphany was received subsequently from the East. It is, in fact, the Eastern Christmas, and Abbot Cabrol refers to it as an "exotic" duplicate of Christmas in the Roman Liturgy. I would suggest that we need not be put off the Epiphany, so to speak, by this remark and I shall suggest later that Dom Casel's emphasis on this feast is altogether proper and necessary, that the Epiphany is the culmination of the Christmas cycle.

That the year should be broken up into these two cycles, these rising and falling movements, seems at first a rather untidy arrangement. The Liturgy climbs twice up double-peaked mountains, as it were, Christmas and the Epiphany, Easter and Pentecost, and then seems to sink down to less exciting levels on the other side of them. Perhaps we ought to regard the first cycle as a sort of trial run, rehearsal or (if I may say so without seeming flippant) approach-shot in respect of the second. To look at it in that way should not lessen its importance in our eyes; rather the contrary. Easter and Pentecost are the definitive climax, but we shall not realize that this is so unless we are prepared for them by the first cycle. And this brings us to the point which Dame Emiliana chiefly stresses in her own introduction to *The Year of Our Lord*: that the mystery is so rich and so far beyond our comprehension in its totality that it must be spread out for us over the whole year, so that we may gradually assimilate it more and more. The Christian cycle is one and unchanging, a *totum simul*, only for the Blessed in heaven who see it in the Beatific Vision. For us it must be seen through the veils of the sacred texts and symbols, distributed to us piecemeal. So Dame Emiliana concludes her essay with a reflexion like that of Dom Casel's about the sacramentals: that God's presence is revealed to us by the very words of the Liturgy; God's voice, heard in the Scriptures and in the Church's formularies, brings us healing and so performs within us the work of our salvation.

Obviously I cannot attempt to provide in a book of this kind a comprehensive account of the way in which the Christian Mystery is articulated in the Missal. All I can do is to point out

[1] This is a controversial matter. It is also maintained that the year began in March.

a few of the characteristics of the liturgical seasons which seem to call for special mention in the context built up by the previous chapters.[1] In turning, then, to the texts of the Advent Masses, we shall not be embarking on a continuous commentary, but on a series of remarks upon a small number of selected passages.

The Mass for the first Sunday in Advent expresses our longing for Christ by using the twenty-fourth psalm for both Introit and Offertory; for the Communion antiphon it uses another psalm which is specially assigned to Advent, the eighty-fourth, which expresses God's answer to our appeal. In turning to the proper prayers, the Collect, the Secret and the Post-Communion, I should like to take the opportunity of offering an opinion on the somewhat vexed question of the way in which they should be rendered in the vernacular. It seems to me that such renderings should be, first and foremost, in a language which can be *prayed*, that is, a language which is not only pure and dignified but also living and simple. But it is surely most desirable that there should be at the same time an attempt to show how the Latin gets there, to help those who are trying to pick up the Latin of the Missal by making the rendering correspond as far as possible with the exact sense and structure of the original. I do not propose to enter here into the question of a vernacular liturgy, but I should like to urge that if there is such a thing as Catholic education it must include instruction in the Ordinary of the Mass *in the Latin*. I cannot see that this is too much to ask; the children may not understand Latin grammar and syntax, but they can surely be sufficiently familiarized with the Latin text (side by side with an English translation) to know at least approximately what English word stands for what Latin word. And, if this be so, the arguments for a vernacular *Ordinary* (I am not speaking of any other part of the Liturgy) are considerably weakened.

After having rashly dogmatized on the delicate matter of translation, I am obliged to take the still more dangerous step of trying to put my principles into practice. Here, then, with much trepidation, I offer versions of the prayers for the First Sunday of Advent:

[1] In what follows I am greatly indebted to the writers above mentioned, Dame Emiliana, Abbot Cabrol and Dom Pius Parsch.

The Collect:

Lord, rouse your power, we pray, and come; that we may deserve by your protection to be rescued from the threatening dangers of our sins and by your deliverance to be made free from them.

Excita quaesumus, Domine, potentiam tuam et veni: ut ab imminentibus peccatorum nostrorum periculis, te mereamur protegente eripi, te liberante salvari.

The Secret Prayer:

May these oblations make us, Lord, come purer, cleansed by their strong power, to their own fountain-head.

Haec sacros nos, Domine, potenti virtute mundatos, ad suum faciant puriores venire principium.

The Post-Communion:

Lord, may we embrace your mercy in the midst of your temple, that we may herald with due honours the coming festival of our renewing.

Suscipiamus, Domine, misericordiam tuam in medio templi tui: ut reparationis nostrae ventura solemnia congruis honoribus praecedamus.

(At the end of this cycle, on the Feast of the Purification, we use the same words from the forty-seventh psalm but with a change of tense, and mood: "We have embraced your mercy.") In the Epistle, St Paul, writing to the Romans, helps us to appreciate the spirit of Advent which breathes in the prayers. It is a time of warning; we have to prepare ourselves not only for the celebration of Christ's birthday but for his Second Advent at the day of Judgment. Unless we bear in mind this double strand of meaning which runs throughout the Liturgy at this time we shall be much baffled. Moreover, Christ is envisaged by the Liturgy as being already—mystically—our Judge. He must first come to us in that capacity, showing us our sins and purifying us from them before we can relive his Incarnation. The Gospel (according to St Luke) which records Christ's solemn and mysterious words about the coming of God's Kingdom, warning us of wrath to come yet urging us to lift up our heads for our redemption is approaching, threatening us with cosmic upheavals yet assuring us that the summer is nigh, strikes precisely the two notes which are to echo through the Advent season: the stern note of penitence and the lyrical note of joyous expectation. This gives to the Advent Liturgy a peculiar charm and richness. It has been called the most "poetical" of the seasons, by which expression presumably our attention is being directed also the abundance of its imagery. But there is another reason for the tone, colour, depth, or whatever one ought to call it, which makes it so attractive: the theme of our Lady, so often explicit, and even more often implicit at this time. The Advent month is, as we shall see more clearly later, the original month of Mary. On this occasion the *Statio* is of extreme significance; it is at Santa Maria Maggiore, which was rebuilt in A.D. 432 to commemorate the Council of Ephesus and dedicated to the "Mother of God". It is the special Christmas *Statio*.

The Mass for the Second Sunday in Advent introduces us to the other two personages who preside, as it were, over the Advent Liturgy: Isaias (in the Introit) and St John the Baptist (in the Gospel). The eighty-fourth psalm reappears at the Offertory, and in the Introit another psalm which belongs specially to Advent appears for the first time, the seventy-ninth. There is no need to show in detail the appropriateness of these psalms; but they must be read and meditated. On this Sunday the emphasis is on joyful anticipation, and again the *Statio*, at the Church of the Holy Cross, the Roman Jerusalem, is of more than historical significance. Jerusalem, for us, is the Kingdom of God, the Church of God, and it is the coming of this New Jerusalem which is celebrated to-day. Yet we are still *preparing* Jerusalem for its King. The Introit and the Gradual speak of his coming to Sion, and the Communion begins stirringly *Jerusalem Surge;* but the proper prayers all insist on the dispositions which must be formed within ourselves.

The Liturgy of the third week of Advent contains some of the most striking compilations in the whole year. There is the combination in the Sunday Mass of lyrical passages from St Paul's Epistle to the Philippians and from Isaias, reinforced by a further and fuller use of the eighty-fourth psalm, with the sober insistence on petition, a combination symbolized by the rose-coloured frontal and vestments, and perfectly expressed by the Collect: "Bend your ear, we pray you, Lord, to our prayers, and enlighten the darkness of our minds with the grace of your visitation." (The Secret Prayer is particularly noteworthy for the almost untranslatable words *devotionis nostrae ... hostia ... immoletur*: "may the victim of our devotion be offered" and *Salutare tuum in nobis ... operetur*: "may it work in us your salvation".) Then there is the Wednesday Mass, the *Missa Aurea* or Golden Mass, as it is called, *Rorate caeli desuper*, celebrating the Annunciation; St Bernard's famous homilies *Super Missus est* were occasioned by its Gospel *missus est Angelus Gabriel*. The Gospel of the Friday Mass puts before us our Lady's visit to St Elizabeth, the Post-Communion praying that once we have been purged of the old man (*a vetustate purgatos*) we may "pass into the fellowship of the saving mystery". And in this week too begin the splendid Vesper chants, the great O antiphons of the Magnificat in which the Gregorian chant expresses the Church's sentiments of longing with an almost uncanny effectiveness.

The Ember Day Mass *Rorate Caeli* will repay some further consideration. The *two* lessons from Isaias show us that it is of great antiquity. Ember days are in fact more ancient than Advent, belonging to the primitive arrangement of Wednesday and Friday *Synaxes*. It would seem that they were originally thanksgivings for the harvests of corn, wine and oil, the most important natural symbols of the Liturgy, as Dom Parsch observes. They were what we should call nowadays "days of recollection"—not so much days of penitence as days of *offering*, associated particularly with almsgiving. (The Ember Saturday of this week acquired a special character owing to the ordinations which were fixed for the occasion; thus it is a day when the Church prays for good priests.) When the Ember Days became a part of Advent their significance naturally underwent a development, so that they are now days of special preparation for Christmas. The *Statio* is once again at Santa Maria Maggiore. The theme of Christ's birth now becomes explicit. Another psalm specially connected with Advent, the eighteenth, is used for the Introit. If we turn to it, we shall find that it portrays Christ as the Sun of Justice setting out upon his course. In the first Gradual the twenty-third psalm, sung to a chant of great beauty, pictures us, dramatically enough, standing outside the closed gates of the earthly paradise and clamouring for the barriers to be lifted. The antiphons consist of the most pointed and exciting prophetic texts from Isaias, the perfect framework for the Gospel of the Annunciation. It is not surprising that they are taken up again for the Introit and the Communion of the Fourth Sunday in Advent and for the Advent Votive Mass of our Lady, which is in fact throughout an adaptation of the Mass *Rorate*. Nor is it surprising that this Mass has been a focus of intense popular devotion. In German-speaking countries it is still celebrated in the winter's dawn, and the faithful make their way to it with lanterns in their hands. White vestments are used; the whole scene vividly represents man's emergence from the darkness into the light of Christ. And the whole Mass emphasizes that in the Advent season Mary is in an especial way our guide and model.

The fourth week of Advent used to begin with our Saturday Ember Mass, which it will be convenient to consider as it originally was, the Mass celebrated at the close of the Saturday vigil, that is to say, first thing on the Sunday morning. The present Sunday Mass, an assemblage of existing Advent texts, came into being when the original one was put back to the Saturday. The present arrangement has this advantage, that those who cannot come to Mass during the week will find on the Sunday all the great themes of the Ember Day Masses, not excluding that of the ordinations, which appears in the Epistle. The theme of the Ember Saturday Mass is that of an *immediate* preparation. It is a solemn summing-up of the whole Advent season, and its importance is underlined by the *Statio*—St Peter's. The symbolism of the night changing into day runs through it. The seventy-ninth and eighteenth psalms are lavishly utilized. The four lessons from Isaias are accompanied by prayers for God's grace of powerful simplicity. The fifth, on this as on Ember Saturdays at other times of the year, is the story from the Book of Daniel of the three young men in the fiery furnace. This, says Dom Parsch, constituted the hour of Lauds in the vigiliary office and symbolized the Resurrection. The great hymn with which the passage ends, *Benedictus es Domine Deus patrum nostrorum*, is, in the context of the Vigils, peculiarly impressive. And when in the Gospel St John the Baptist has been shown to us as fulfilling Isaias's prophecy that every valley shall be filled and every mountain and hill brought low, all is now ready. But before we leave the Liturgy of Advent for that of Christmas we are reminded by the Epistle of this Mass that it was the Second Advent which was chiefly before the minds of the early Christians, for we find here the words of warning addressed by St Paul to the Thessalonians.

We may now pass in very rapid review the Masses of Christmas and of the Epiphany. The custom of celebrating three Masses at Christmas originated in Jerusalem. The faithful met for Mass at night in the grotto of the Nativity, and on their return to Jerusalem, since it was by now the hour of the Resurrection, naturally celebrated another Mass at the Church of the Resurrection (with the shepherds of the Nativity specially in mind). Later in the day there was also a solemn celebration. In Rome this procedure was closely imitated. The first and third Masses are now at Santa Maria Maggiore, the second at the Roman Church of the Resurrection. Originally the third was at St Peter's. It may be useful to concentrate for the most part upon two themes which appear prominently in these Christmas Masses: the theme of light and the theme of Redemption. It would be a mistake, as we have seen earlier, to regard the two as separate. Christ is the Saviour *because* he is the Light of the World; he heals by teaching and teaches by healing, so we must not countenance violent contrasts between the Eastern and Western ways of regarding the divine economy—for both East and West (with differences which are only matters of emphasis) the Word saves us from the double darkness of ignorance and of sin. In these three Masses we can trace a progression in our emergence. In the midnight Mass there is, so to speak, a spotlight revealing the divine Child with only one other human being, his Mother. In the second Mass, the rising of the sun shows him to us, represented by the shepherds, as our Saviour. The third embraces the whole scope of the Redemptive mystery, which is now starting to unfold, from the eternal birth of the uncreated Word to his universal sway over the hearts of his human brethren.

Christmas, then, is a feast of light. The date is itself a proof of it. It is not, historically considered, the actual date of Christ's birth (which we do not know), but the feast of the winter solstice of the Christian Sun God, the *Sol Invictus*. The first prayer of the first Mass speaks of the "true light", and prays that we may be led to heaven by our knowledge of the "mysteries of this light". The Secret and Post-Communion prayers, the only parts of the Mass which do not refer explicitly to this theme, place it in its most profoundly significant setting, the Secret asking that through these most holy transactions (*sacrosancta commercia*) we may be found in Christ's perfect likeness (*forma*), now that he has become one with us in substance (*substantia*), the Post-Communion reverting to the theme of the "mysteries" through which we are to grow in fellowship with him. The Second Mass, *in aurora*, known as the Mass of the Shepherds, an exceptionally lovely composition which is too little known to the faithful, is a series of brilliant coruscations of light. *Lux fulgebit* are its opening words—"the light shall break forth with splendour". *Luce perfundimur*, the Collect goes on; "we are drenched in this light"; and it concludes in mystical language of unsurpassed grandeur: "may that which breaks forth with splendour in our intellects (*fulget in mente*) shine out in our lives" (*resplendeat opere*). Again it is the Secret prayer which from its central point of vantage produces the most *comprehensive* formula: *Sicut homo genitus idem refulsit et Deus, sic nobis haec terrena substantia conferat quod divinum est* (the rhythm of this must not be missed)—"as he born as a man blazed forth, he who is God, one and the same [a clumsy attempt, I fear, to render *idem et Deus*], so may this earthly substance (the offerings) give us the divine." In the third Mass the Sun is high in the heavens, illuminating the whole world. *Hodie descendit lux magna*, we sing in the verse of the Alleluia, *Viderunt omnes fines terrae*, in the Communion. And the Gospel marks the climax, for it is St John's prologue: *Erat lux vera quae illuminat omnem hominem venientem in hunc mundum*. The enemies of Christ naturally look with special loathing at the candles burning on the Christmas tree.

The development of the theme of light has been at the same

time a development of the theme of Redemption. Only one or two details need be added to show how in the Liturgy, and especially in the Christmas Liturgy, the contemplative aspect of our religion is indistinguishable from the ascetic, the intellectual from the moral. The coming of Christ to our hearts is, if only we will permit it, the death of sin. In all the three Christmas Epistles St Paul tells us to remember what Christ has done for us, that he has given himself on our behalf "to cleanse for himself an acceptable people"—redemption is his doing; our task is only to take the obstacles out of his way. His marvellous birth, says the Post-Communion of the Aurora Mass, has abolished our decrepitude (*repulit vetustatem*). It is to free us from the slavery of sin, according to the Collect of the third Mass. The psalm *De profundis*, which may seem so unsuitable for Christmas Vespers, was apparently chosen because of the phrase *copiosa apud eum redemptio*.

The Mass *Dum medium silentium*, for the Sunday within the Octave and the vigil of the Epiphany, carries on the theme of the Redemption, and is at the same time a bridge between the two great feasts of the first cycle and a sort of first suggestion or advance notice of the second. On the Vigil the Gospel tells us of the return of the Holy Family from Egypt, the setting forth having been described on the Feast of the Holy Innocents. This is the place for pointing out that the Roman Liturgy celebrates *historical* Feasts (that of the Circumcision, for example, during this season), whereas the Eastern Feast of the Epiphany was originally supra-historical and contained no reference to the visit of the Magi. Thus the Roman Liturgy has brought the Feast into its own system. But it has not thereby destroyed its sublimity. The Feast of the Manifestation, which in respect of its privileged Octave is superior to Christmas, ought to be for us, as indeed it really is, the final triumph of the whole cycle. The Western mind, it must be confessed, has not taken to it as kindly as one might wish. Perhaps—dare I say?—it has not been sufficiently *preached*. At the Epiphany we celebrate the recognition by the world of Christ as God. Not to realize that Christmas *leads* to this is to confuse means with ends. It may even be a sign of a certain sentimentalism, a superficiality which fails in some degree to appreciate the essence of Christianity.

We see here a clear example of the way in which the Liturgy is a true school of saints. It is by revealing himself to us as God that Christ our brother unites us with the Father, the Son and the Holy Ghost, bestowing upon us the gift of faith, the beginning of eternal life. In the Roman Liturgy of the Epiphany we celebrate the first *miracles* through which this revelation was conveyed to the world at large, the star which guided the Magi, the first fruits of the faith, the miracle at Cana, the most patently "mystical" of all our Lord's "signs", and the voice which was heard at his baptism by John in the Jordan, "this is my well-beloved Son".

We may call the Mass of the Epiphany "exotic" only if we are prepared to qualify Christianity itself by this adjective. In a proper sense it is indeed perfectly applicable, that is if we take it to mean that the good news of Christianity is a pure gift of God, surpassing man's wildest dreams. It is the transformation of humanity, but a transformation in which nothing is destroyed. This Mass, as Dom Parsch observes, may be taken as a classical model. The seventy-first psalm, the *royal* psalm *par excellence*, is used for the Processions. And the Processions to-day are of the fullest possible significance. At the Introit we greet Christ in the person of the celebrant. He comes as an oriental sovereign to the accompaniment of illuminations and acclamations, and he prepares for the inhabitants of the favoured city a royal feast. But this is also a bridal feast, and so first we offer our gifts to him—the Offertory, the Procession of the Magi, of all the redeemed, is to-day the prototype Offertory. The *Statio* is naturally St Peter's. The Collect gives definitive utterance to he theme of light: the star of faith has led us to Christ, and we pray that we may be led at last to behold the beauty of his heavenly glory (*speciem celsitudinis*). The Secret prayer identifies the Epiphany gifts with Christ himself: it is a piece of the purest sacramental theology, a perfect balance of thought and expression, about which a whole essay might be written. The journey of the Magi is the picture of the whole Christian life, a life of pilgrimage, threatened by the power of this world. But the end is also the way, for Christ, the day-star, leads us to himself— *purificatae mentis intelligentia consequamur* "may we follow after him with the understanding of a purified mind", says the

Post-Communion prayer. We offer him in the gold, the frankincense and the myrrh, our love, our adoration and our suffering. The prophecy of Isaias, the subject of the Epistle, is thus fulfilled in the Gospel of the Magi. The Gradual and the Alleluia effect the transition from the one to the other, the first repeating the theme of the gifts in the *Surge et illuminare, Jerusalem,* the second using the words of the Gospel to the same effect. In the Communion antiphon this verse *Vidimus stellam* is used once more, for now we are prostrated, like the Magi, before the Son of God, hidden within us beneath the eucharistic species; now his Manifestation is consummated.

VII

THE LITURGICAL YEAR: II: THE PASCHAL CYCLE

I N THIS CHAPTER I PROPOSE FIRST TO INDICATE THE WAY IN which the Liturgy works up towards Holy Week, then to draw your attention to a few of the texts for the Holy Week functions, and lastly to suggest that the final phase of the Paschal Liturgy has not won the appreciation which it deserves relatively to the Triduum Sanctum, which has thrown it, I think, somewhat into the shade.

It is useless to pretend that the present arrangement of the Roman Missal presents us with a consistently ordered sequence. Originally, no doubt, the passages from the Sacred Scriptures were arranged continuously; now we can observe the traces of this only at certain seasons. The use made of the Psalter gave a uniform character to the Mass of the day; so often did the *Statio*. The Proper of each Mass was a composition of inter-related themes; modern attempts to unearth such themes from our Missal, and even to reduce the whole text of a Proper to a single theme, suffer perhaps sometimes from over-ingenuity. But it would be a far worse mistake to regard the Missal as a mere hotchpotch. There is a great deal left which belongs to what we may call the classical period of Mass-composition. And the structure of the calendar, as regards the commemoration of the historical events of our Lord's life, is substantially intact.

As soon as we pass onwards from the Feast of the Epiphany we come across an exception to the general rule just enunci-ated. The Octave of the Epiphany ended with the celebration of Christ's baptism in the Jordan. And the Sunday in this Octave naturally commemorated the Finding in the Temple, the only event known in our Lord's boyhood, in order to effect the transition between his infancy and his public ministry. But the Feast of the Holy Family, putting before us a meditation on our Lord's hidden life rather than commemorating a period of time, nowadays (since 1921) takes the place of the Sunday within the Octave, the Mass of which is postponed to the next free day. These two Masses provide an interesting contrast between the modern style and the ancient. The modern Mass has a direct and particular moral purpose: to sanctify family life. It makes a direct appeal to the emotions. It is connected only in the loosest way with the Office of the Feast, and is of a discursive nature. The ancient Mass, on the other hand, always keeps in view the Christian Mystery which it is re-presenting. Its immediate appeal is to the intelligence. And its language is objective, hieratic, universal. The Mass for the Sunday within the Octave of the Epiphany considers the Finding in the Temple as a divine manifestation, a phase of Christ's redemptive activity. The event which it commemorates is the first recorded utterance of the Incarnate Word, his declaration of his divine mission, which is at the same time his first hint of his divinity. The Introit antiphon is eminently suitable for the time. It describes Christ upon his throne, surrounded by his angels, and speaks of the eternity of his reign. And the psalm is the great psalm of the Resurrection, the ninety-ninth, reminding us of the significance of Sunday. The eschatological character of the Introit (*In excelso throno*) has suggested that we should look at the Finding in the Temple as itself of eschatological significance, and Dom Parsch invites us to consider our Lady as standing here for the Church who seeks with longing for her absent Lord and finds him at last with joy. Thus the Mass would show him to us as attaining his majority both in his first and in his second Advent. The Collect is faithful to the central theme, the accomplishment of the Father's will. In the Epistle we hear St Paul's exhortation to offer our bodies as living victims, holy and acceptable to God (the gifts of the Magi are still in mind, perhaps). The Offertory antiphon stresses the joy with which we should so present ourselves, and the Communion antiphon, by repeating the operative words of the Gospel, urges us again to apply them to ourselves. The Secret prayer conforms to the classcial type: "may the sacrifice offered to you, Lord, both quicken us always and defend us".

The Masses for the Sundays after Epiphany expand and comment upon the theme of *Theophany*, with suggestions of that contest between the light and the darkness which is to be the subject of so many of the Lenten Masses. The Mass for the second Sunday is altogether bound up with the Epiphany, since its Gospel records the marriage at Cana. We must not look at the miracles of Jesus merely as historical events. When we hear the words of the Gospel, they are being addressed to us now (P. Bouyer in his recently published Life of St Antony has given a most valuable account of the Saint's conversion from this point of view). The miracles are redemptive; that is, they belong to the universal divine economy—they are for *our* salvation. *We* are the wedding-guests of Cana, and what Christ accomplished on this particular occasion is a symbol of what he accomplishes in the Mass to-day. That, as we have seen, is why the singing of the Gospel is accompanied by so much significant ceremonial. And that is why the Communion antiphon here makes use of the words of the Gospel. For this is in truth that good wine which has been saved until now. (The mystical significance of the changing of water into wine has been exploited to the full by the Fathers.) The sixty-fifth psalm, which is used both for the Introit and the Offertory, is really a Paschal canticle; but the note of exultant adoration is equally fitting during the Epiphany season. So is the hundred-and-sixth which appears for the Gradual, with its reference to the sending of God's Word. The prayers have no peculiar appositeness; the Secret and Post-Communion are formulas: the Collect was probably a sort of *oratio imperata* or prayer for some special occasion of great danger. But the special character of the Mass as a marriage feast is preserved.

The Third Sunday after the Epiphany is the last of this series in that its antiphons are simply repeated on the fourth, fifth and sixth Sundays (in years in which these occur). The historical sequence of the events of our Lord's life has already ended, all these Sundays being concerned with our Lord's miracles and teachings without regard to their chronological order. The Gospels are taken for the time being from that according to St Matthew and from the eighth and thirteenth chapters, a relic presumably of the system of continuous readings. The ninety-sixth psalm, the psalm of royal judgment, predominates, showing that the Epiphany has not been left behind. It describes the Lord appearing in the majesty of a storm, bringing light to the just and terror to the unjust. The Offertory, too, speaks of the might of his right hand, using the hundred and seventeenth psalm, the Paschal psalm of the Resurrection, probably with the Gospel in mind (the stretching forth of our Lord's hand to heal the leper). The Collect is a prayer for the stretching forth of God's hand to succour our weakness. The Gospel also records the healing of the centurion's servant, and we are reminded that, as we hear his words whenever we come to Holy Communion, we should share his faith and his dispositions. Our Lord has himself connected the miracle with Holy Communion by his own words on this occasion about the coming of the Gentiles to the heavenly banquet. By putting before us this passage also, the text of this Mass plainly declares its general purport: to celebrate the entrance of Gentiles and sinners into the Kingdom of God, the further manifestation of Christ's power.

In the other Sunday Masses of this season, the only fresh features are the prayers and the passages chosen from Sacred Scripture. The Gospels show us Christ successively as the Victor, stilling the storm on the lake, as the Judge, in the parable of the good seed and the cockle, and as the Lord of the harvest in the parables of the mustard-seed and the leaven. The Epistles are concerned with the building up of God's kingdom by charity and the virtues of the Christian life. The Introit, Offertory and Communion antiphons remain the same, but they seem to gain fresh significance in their various contexts; this may be the result of accident, but, although we may speak of the relative "poverty" of the Liturgy at this season, we need not complain of it. Nor is it to depreciate the prayers of the Proper to say simply that they conform to regular types. The last Post-Communion deserves quotation in what must be a very literal and "bumpy" English version: "now that we are fed with your heavenly delights, grant, Lord, that we may always have an appetite for these same things by which we truly live."

With Septuagesima Sunday we enter the furthest fringe of the Paschal cycle. The three weeks season which it begins, a bridge between Epiphany and Lent, came into being relatively late, about the time of St Gregory. The original careful arrangement has remained practically fixed. It is on the whole a rather gloomy season, gloomier, I was about to say, than Lent—but that would have been a lapse, because Lent is not gloomy at all. The fact seems to be that the Masses of Septuagesima and Sexagesima, in particular, reflect the very threatening political conditions of the 6th century (which makes them extraordinarily appropriate for the middle of the 20th). On Septuagesima Sunday the tone is established by the seventeenth psalm ("the groans of death surrounded me") and the hundred and twenty-ninth, the *De profundis*, a cry for mercy. In the Epistle St Paul warns the Corinthians of their need to struggle manfully, and the Gospel (the hiring of the workers for the vineyard) ends with the words "many are called, but few chosen". The framework of the Sexagesima Mass is similar in character, but the Collect, the Epistle and the Gospel refer to the *Statio* (St Paul's-outside-the-walls); this Sunday is in fact the original feast of St Paul (that of January 25th originating in the 10th century)—the Epistle is the long passage in Second Corinthians in which St Paul speaks of his hardships and his mystical experiences, and the Gospel, suitably enough, contains the parable of the Sower. Quinquagesima Sunday has rather a less desolate air about it. We have again a long passage from St Paul in the Epistle, but this time it is the great hymn of charity: the Gospel, St Luke's account of the cure of the blind beggar, begins with our Lord's announcement of his Passion and Resurrection. The Introit and the Tract, particularly fine examples of the Gregorian chant, sound a note of confidence which will become familiar to us during Lent.

At this point my already highly selective method of comment will become more selective still. I deliberately avoid speaking at any length of the Lenten Masses and the ceremonies of Holy Week because they are relatively familiar to the faithful; popular commentaries on them abound. It is perfectly correct to say that the Lenten Masses are penitential. But we must not overlook the fact that the Church's Liturgy never allows us to lose sight of the *purpose* of penance—to fit us for a life of union with God. The theme of the first fortnight of Lent is Christ's triumphant combat against the powers of darkness, into which we must enter if we are to be prepared for the glories of Easter.

And let us be clear at the outset that there is no question of *pretending* during Lent that Christ has *not* risen—he is now to "easter" more effectually in *us* through our annual purification. The Mass for the First Sunday in Lent is one of the few which have retained their classical form. The ninetieth psalm, the Compline psalm of confidence in battle, is chanted almost in its entirety in the Tract; the rest of it appears in the other chants, which are all drawn from this same source. In the Epistle the solemn exhortation is addressed to the Church as a whole (Lent ought not to be an individualistic preparation) with the candidates for the Easter baptism specially in mind.

Indeed the scrutinies of the catechumens have exercised a profound influence on the Lenten Liturgy as a whole. The Monday, Wednesday, and Friday Masses nearly always refer to them in some way. Those for the other weekdays are of later date and concern themselves more generally with the themes of the Passion and of the duties of a Christian. In this first week the Wednesday, Friday and Saturday are Ember days. The Wednesday is, in accordance with the rule, consecrated to our Lady (the *Statio* is at Santa Maria Maggiore), and so a day of special recollection. The Saturday Mass was celebrated after the night Vigil, and so has the thanksgiving character which belongs to Sundays. The Mass for the Second Sunday is therefore like that for the Fourth Sunday of Advent, a later compilation for what was originally an a-liturgical day, using the chants of the previous Wednesday and the Gospel of the Saturday. This Gospel, which recounts the Transfiguration on Mount Thabor, is of extreme significance and enables us to trace the fundamental development of the preceding week. On the first Sunday we have witnessed our Lord's fast, his triumph over the devil and the ministry of the Angels. On the Wednesday we hear of the fasts of Moses and Elias, after which Moses receives the Law and Elias reaches the mountain of God. Now Moses and Elias appear on the mountain of the Transfiguration. Fasting, then, prepares us for the service of God and leads us to our final goal, as the Lenten preface points out to us in language of great purity (it seems a pity that our existing laws of fasting should be inapplicable to most of the faithful, for they are thus deprived of a full share in the liturgical celebrations.)

Our union with Christ in his Transfiguration is meant to quicken our faith, to encourage us to enter more deeply and with greater confidence into the Mystery of his Passion. The older Masses of the second week of Lent underline the approach of the conflict between light and darkness, between our Lord and his enemies. In the third week (I am borrowing once more from Dom Parsch) our Lord seems to pass from the defensive to the offensive. The Gospel of the third Sunday, about the strong man who is vanquished by one still stronger, establishes the theme. In the weekday Masses Christ triumphs over evil in his catechumens. Chiefly, in this week, he appears as the healer of the soul (so on the Thursday we have the Mass *Salus populi* in honour of the stational saints, the doctors Cosmas and Damian, and on the Saturday the splendid Mass of the penitents *ad Sanctam Susannam* with the accounts of the innocent Susanna and the repentant adulteress). Dame Emiliana points out how the Liturgy, despite its dramatic theme, introduces us to this week in an "atmosphere of calm content". This is true: the Sunday Mass is shot through with the "joyful contemplation" of Christ's presence, reminding us that in a sense we are already in possession of what we desire.[1] The lovely Communion chant, using the fourth and fifth verses of the eighty-third psalm, is particularly noteworthy in this connexion: "The swallow has found her a house and the turtle a nest where she may lay her young (and I have found) your altars ... blessed are they who dwell in your house ..." On the fourth Sunday this theme is explicit throughout. The Mass *Laetare, Jerusalem* is justly famous. It is the Church's maternal rejoicing over the catechumens, a spring time feast anticipating the joy of Easter. The Gospel (the feeding of the five thousand) gives it an appropriately eucharistic character. And again the Communion antiphon has a movingly lyrical quality: *illuc enim ascenderunt tribus, tribus Domini.*

Even Passiontide is a season of rejoicing. Modern piety concentrates upon the particular historical incidents of our Lord's Passion, considers his virtues and tries to obtain them. There is an emphasis on the truth that Christ died for each one of us and on contrition for our personal offences against him.

[1] *The Year of Our Lord*, p. 119.

The Liturgy is always going behind the historical facts to the *purpose* of the Passion, to the Redemption itself, our salvation. The Holy Father has declared in the Encyclical *Mediator* that we must not *repudiate* the more historical approach of modern piety, and in particular the modern "realistic" crucifix. That being so, it might seem that we should give up the veiling of the crucifix during Passiontide, for what the veil is meant to conceal is the ancient *cross* of precious metal, studded with jewels. That was the way in which the Church used to mourn for her Lord. For of course she does mourn. But her mourning is a *redemptive participation* in Christ's Passion. In Passion Week we enter into the sanctuary with the High Priest who is himself the victim of the sacrifice. The Gospel has been taken from that of St John since the Friday of the third week in Lent; we have heard the wonderful passages about the woman of Samaria, about the healing of the man born blind, about the raising of Lazarus, all strikingly commented upon by the Communion chants. It is still the chosen friend of Christ, the contemplative whose gaze is so direct and so penetrating, who presents him to us in this week. In the first of the Gospels from St John we hear: "my meat is to do the will of him that sent me", and on Passion Sunday the tremendous words: "before Abraham was, I am". Christ as man is our way, and as God he is the truth and the life. Perhaps we might sum up St John's Gospel in those words. And what is this way? The perfect correspondence with God's will, the exact performance of all the duties of our state for the building up of Christ's kingdom on earth—yes, indeed, but this is not all that must be said. How did Christ strike his contemporaries? Surely above all, as a man of prayer, as one who *knew God*. And his teaching to us is that we too, through our union with him, must know God.

I have dispensed myself from offering you even a bird's-eye view of Holy Week. It can be gained from the Introduction to Dr Adrian Fortescue's "Holy Week Book", which should be used in conjunction with the great book of P. Bouyer's on the Paschal Mystery to which I have so often referred in previous connexions. Here are simply a few reflexions which seem to arise naturally at the point which we have now reached. First, we must not allow Holy Week to lose in our minds its integral association with Easter Week. They are the two leaves of a single diptych. The Liturgy of these two weeks, taken, as they should be, together, are a condensation of Christianity: if we have been crucified with Christ, it is that we may live with him. The lesson of the Liturgy is, most simply, Christian sanctity. When we are taking part in the Liturgy we are at the same time both engaging in the fight and rejoicing in the victory—that is to say, we are really *living* as Christians. The Liturgy is a *work*, but one which contains its own reward; in that sense its value is in itself. It is not, fundamentally, a complicated affair. On the contrary, if we can only imbibe the spirit of the Liturgy (and here, at the very heart of it, it should be easiest to do so) we find that it is teaching us *simplicity* (we realize, for example, that asceticism and "humanism" and meditation and contemplation are not after all so many different things). Unless we become as little children we cannot enter the Kingdom of Heaven. We must become, in the end, single-minded.

It may be just a chance but it is, I think, a happy one that the Palm Sunday ceremony begins Holy Week with the children of the Hebrews singing their Hosannas and the Easter Octave ends with the Mass *Quasi modo geniti infantes*. Throughout the Easter Liturgy the thought of the newly baptized predominates. This is not merely an interesting historical reference. It is meant for us all; we are meant to be renewing our baptismal vows. We are going with Christ to the Father. When the subdeacon knocks with the cross on the church-door on Palm Sunday we are entering Jerusalem with our Lord for his Passion. "I, if I be lifted up, will draw all men unto me." The Passion is the tragedy of the Jews but the triumph of Christ. This is not as fully realized as it should be. It is significant that among the functions of Holy Week the para-liturgical function of the Stations of the Cross on Good Friday has, relatively, so great a popularity.

These extremes of tragedy and triumph are put before us most obviously on Maundy Thursday. In the morning we have the joyful commemoration of the Last Supper (and our obedience to Christ's command is accompanied by every circumstance calculated to impress upon us the splendour of the occasion, despite the shadow of Judas's betrayal which falls across it); in the evening we are plunged into the horrors of sin, the desolation of Jerusalem. The ceremony which gives Maundy Thursday its name is perhaps a special opportunity for reminding ourselves that we are not just discharging ritual duties in Holy Week; something is supposed to be happening, to ourselves. The fact that our Lord in the person of the celebrant stoops before a row of little boys does not provide us simply with an *example* of humility. The dramatization is effective in a more direct sense. If we identify ourselves with our Lord, so far as we may, while he washes the feet of his disciples, he bathes our souls there and then in charity. *Gaudium immensum atque probum.* That is what the liturgical drama is to effect.

Even on Good Friday the note of triumph is not absent. At the end of the Reproaches the Church suddenly bursts into praise of the Resurrection—"for behold by the wood of the Cross joy came into the world". The ceremonies of Good Friday teach us sorrow, indeed, but a sorrow which springs from love, and all love is joyful if it is requited (we love our Lord because he first loved us). We shall have this true sorrow for our sins if we as his members unite with him as our Head on the Cross; and we do this by what Abbot Chapman called "an act of inattention " to everything save Christ himself as the rite reveals him. It does reveal him—both on Good Friday and on Holy Saturday, even if we are baffled by particular words and particular symbols. "An educated Catholic" ought to mean someone who isn't baffled. Anyway, if we have shared the simplicity of the naked Christ the previous evening, we shall be ready to see in the striking of the new fire from the flint the irruption of the supernatural. When the deacon holds up the three-branched candle-stick and sings *Lumen Christi*, it will seem inevitably appropriate that we should first kneel and then sing *Deo Gratias*. And when the five grains of incense are placed in the Paschal Candle our souls will be fixed by this image on the mystery of the whole Christ, the *Puer Aeternus* in whom we are made young, the Lamb who was slain, sitting upon a throne.[1]

"Eastertide," says Fr Martindale in his deservedly popular book *The Mind of the Missal*, "is a more difficult period than Passiontide for most people to deal with because there is less in

---

[1] This paragraph is taken from a contribution to the *Bulletin of the League of Christ the King* for March 1946.

it that appeals to the imagination. And perhaps tragedy is always more enthralling than joy."[1] Perhaps we may distinguish here between different kinds of joy. The joy of Easter is the specifically Christian kind: the rejoicing over Christ's victory—surely we may expect people to appreciate this. It is a further conquest of our heritage, another stage of our growth in Christ: it is a contemplative joy, but by no means to be regarded on that account as a luxury of the few; and it ought to be more enthralling than anything else. Let us turn back for a moment or two to the Blessing of the New Fire and the *Exsultet* on Holy Saturday, in which the Liturgy is wholly joyful, and consider some of its phrases. We have to exert our imaginations a little to realize that this is really a Vigil. But when we have done so, we can hardly fail to be impressed, even overwhelmed. All the lights are out when the ceremony begins, and in the first prayer our Lord is called the cornerstone which has brought the fire of God's brightness to the faithful. Then we have a sort of meditation on fire, darting brilliantly and erratically in all directions. The second prayer calls God the author (*conditor*) of all lights, and takes us back to Moses and the coming-forth from Egypt; for this *is* the Phase, the *Transitus Domini*, the opening of the Red Sea and the opening of heaven, for both are bound up with and depend upon the opening of the tomb. The writer of the third prayer could not resist bringing in the fiery darts of the evil one, as if to remind us that symbolism, so to speak, cuts both ways, that life is always exciting one way or the other, that if we are not burnt up with love we shall find ourselves being burnt up with hate. When the five grains of incense are blessed, the prayer says nothing of the five wounds which the glorious Body bears. And perhaps this is just as well. What it does say defies commentary. *Veniat ... larga tuae benedictionis infusio; et hunc nocturnum splendorem invisibilis regenerator accende.* It goes on so majestically, *sacrificium, quod hac nocte litatum est, arcana luminis tui admixtione refulgeat* that it seems to be almost its own answer when it concludes *virtus tuae majestatis assistat.*

The *Exsultet* (nowadays attributed to St Ambrose) has won much admiration. But in a thing of such many-sided beauty

[1] p. 134. (In this and the following paragraphs I am drawing on an article contributed to *Music and Liturgy* for April 1941 and April 1943.)

there is room for plenty of anthologies. It is worth noticing, for example, that the endings of the periods have generally in a most marked degree that unforgettable quality which characterizes great poetry. Before the grains of incense are placed in the Candle we have the following:—

> *Totius orbis se sentiat amisisse caliginem* . . .
> *Veteris piaculi cautionem pio cruore detersit* . . .
> *Fugat odia, concordiam parat et curvat imperia* . . .

This is the passage which contains what are perhaps the best-known phrases: the deacon's reference to himself, breaking the otherwise inviolate rule of Roman impersonality; the series of exclamations ending with *O felix culpa* and *O vere beata nox* and the repetitions of *haec nox est.* But what follows is still more marvellous.

The Deacon has sung *Sed iam columnae huius praeconia novimus, quam in honorem Dei rutilans ignis accendit.* He lights the Candle and adds a few lines which have not attracted perhaps the attention which they deserve: *Qui licet sit divisus in partes, mutuati tamen luminis detrimenta non novit. Alitur enim liquantibus ceris, quas in substantiam pretiosae huius lampadis apis mater eduxit.* The rhythmical balance and effortless grace of this have not gone unnoticed; nor has the tenderness of *apis mater* at the close, a sort of overflowing of charity upon unknowing creatures. But has not the meditation on fire reached a climax here? Fire is something which consumes, but is not itself consumed, which has the power to kindle for so long as there is matter for its kindling. It is the business of wax to be annihilated at the contact of the flame. It is the business of man to be passive to God's action. Our God (at Easter we celebrate Christ's Godhead) is a consuming fire.

One of the most astounding things about what follows is that anything follows. This storm of praise seems to have blown itself out into a quiet, almost a Pindaric, ending. But now, with the lighting of the lamps, there is a fresh gust. Indeed, except that there is nothing hysterical about it, we might call it a hurricane, the more overpowering in that it is so unexpected. *O vere beata nox, quae exspoliavit Aegyptios, ditavit Hebraeos. Nox, in qua terrenis caelestia, humanis divina iunguntur.* The anaphora is more breathless. It is *nox* now, no longer *haec est nox*. And as the final climax appears, the resources of human language, which seemed to have been utterly exhausted, put forth an endeavour in which they seem to be shedding their mortal vesture and disappearing, lifted by their aspiration into the very realm of spirit. *Flammas eius lucifer matutinus inveniat. Ille, inquam, lucifer, qui nescit occasum.* But this is no vague illuminism; it is the Christian fact. *Ille, qui regressus ab inferis, humano generi serenus illuxit.*

Easter Sunday is the "ordinary" Liturgy most conscious of its sublimity because in the closest contact with its source. The point is that instead of sinking to an "ordinary" level we should realize that the Liturgy is never "ordinary", if by that we mean dull. St Benedict says that his monks should consider all seasons as Lent; the counterpart is that we should consider them all as Easter. The beginning of the Sunday Mass is a roll of thunder: *Resurrexi et adhuc tecum sum, alleluia; posuisti super me manum tuam, alleluia.* There are ten "u" sounds in a dozen words. In the first dozen words of the Gospel there is only one: *In illo tempore: Maria Magdalene, et Maria Jacobi, et Salome emerunt aromata.* This is the lightness of the dawn. The same thing happens in the Sequence (which is "dramatic", if anything is): *Dic nobis, Maria, quid vidisti in via?*, and at the end of it the "u" sounds return in force mixed with the excited penetrating "i" ones: *Scimus Christum surrexisse a mortuis vere.* The Introit for Wednesday has this quality: *Venite, benedicti Patris mei, percipite regnum, alleluia; quod vobis paratum est ab origine mundi, alleluia, alleluia, alleluia.* And the rise of the Gregorian chant at *ab origine* is as really dramatic, if less obviously, as the Sequence. I have not the space I should like to quote from the prayers. They are too little known and too seldom used. Turn for example to the Collect for Monday, the Post-Communion for Tuesday and the Secret for Saturday. They are typical of the deep but clear theology and the sustained magnificence of language which marks this week.

We are never allowed to forget that this is the Feast of feasts. *Pascha nostrum immolatus est Christus* answers to and fulfils *Verbum caro factum est.* The Introits take up the theme unceasingly: *Introduxit vos Dominus in terram fluentem lac et mel, alleluia* (Monday); *Aqua sapientiae potavit eos, alleluia* (Tuesday). The neophytes keep on coming in: *Linguas infantium fecit disertas, alleluia* (Tuesday) and the Communion antiphon *Populus acquisitionis* (Thursday). The last is from St Peter whose first Epistle begins to appear, providing what might be called the philosopher's Introit (already mentioned) for Low Sunday: *Quasi modo geniti infantes, alleluia; rationabiles, sine dolo lac concupiscite, alleluia, alleluia, alleluia.* Again the extraordinary delicacy of sound appears. The theologian St Paul rightly had pride of place for the Epistle on Easter Day itself. But there is in St Peter as in St John (who also comes to the fore just now) something which drives it home to us that they had drunk at the Source, that they had known him in the flesh. It is not only that they say so, but that they break out into a spontaneous enthusiasm which seems to take us back with them.

Fr Martindale, after stressing the inarticulate joy of the Easter Alleluias, goes on: "… the actual words of much of these Masses seem, sometimes, pale and unimaginative".[1] Bright lights are pale in a way, white being the absence of colour. But it seems odd to characterize the Easter Masses in this fashion, especially when the writer adds: "On the other hand, there is a strong impression of primitiveness in these Masses. They live in the world of the Acts, of St Peter and St John." The notes of Easter Week are those which raise our minds most effectively to the thought of God. The ideas of light and peace, freshness and activity, power and majesty, abundance of life and overflowing generosity are everywhere.

We may fittingly end by recalling to our minds the recognition-scenes put before us by the Gospels of this week: "Were not our hearts burning within us as he spoke to us in the way?" … "Jesus said to her 'Mary'."[2] "So that disciple whom Jesus loved said to Peter 'It is the Lord' ".

---

[1] *The Mind of the Missal*, p. 141.
[2] Since this chapter was written the Holy See has authorized the celebration of the Easter Vigil at the appropriate time and with modifications which help to bring home to the faithful its deepest significance. This is an event of great importance and of a most encouraging kind.

VIII

THE LITURGICAL YEAR : III : PENTECOST

A LIST OF QUOTATIONS FROM THE MISSAL, EVEN IF THEY ARE strung together by some threads of argument, easily becomes wearisome to follow. So I shall interrupt for a few minutes this very jerky progress through the Liturgical Year to develop a line of thought which was indicated in the previous lecture about the *language* of the Liturgy. And again I ask leave to quote from work already published:[1] "There is an apologetic field here, for the average classical scholar or man of letters is still largely unaware of these supreme achievements of the Latin tongue. 'Supreme achievements' needs some justifying. People look askance nowadays at general statements about literature and at 'essays in appreciation'. But this is partly because they have no scheme of values; for Catholics, who have, it is important to see where literature comes in. We have our standpoints more or less, in other fields, but here we still seem groping. 'Appreciation', however sound, may seem a mere parade of sensibility; but if we think we can point to what is good, we need not be ashamed to do so.

"There seem to be two ways of looking at literature. We can concentrate on the element of beauty, and then we seem to be looking at the result of a peculiar skill in the manipulation of words, based on an intelligence keener than most to perceive their associations: unities of many kinds, combining to produce an intelligible content which we find full and satisfying. What you say and the way in which you say it can hardly be sifted clear from one another, but these two sides of the thing do obviously exist and here the second one is uppermost. The discovery of unities in and for themselves is a valuable and important thing, for we perceive laws in words or sounds (or colours and shapes, it may be) more easily and more immediately (and so more keenly and enjoyably) than the laws of thought itself, the unity behind everything which is really God himself; and it

[1] In *Music and Liturgy*, April 1943, pp. 39 and 40.

is useful for us to stretch the mind like this and makes us realize its nature, the illimitability of its desires. It is the fashion nowadays to refer to the values of literature in terms of feeling. But clearly we must relate them to what is most important in us, to our intellects. We are considering something typically human; it must not sink to any lower level, nor must it lose itself in a false mysticism.

"But when we think of the element of beauty in literature we are concentrating only on one side of it, though one which may be, I should say (others would differ), the main part of it—as, for example, in some of Shakespeare's lyrics. When we speak of literary greatness we generally mean something more than this though bound up with it—a wider revelation of reality, something worth knowing about ourselves and the world we live in, nothing new (perhaps) but a clearer view of it. From this standpoint we are no longer concentrating on the form of expression for its own sake; we are looking at it for the value expressed. If the liturgy expresses man's relations with God it follows that it must be the highest of human arts. It might be argued that it does not express them with that direct and vivid relation which is requisite for literary excellence. It might be argued too that these reactions are spurious. We should expect these objections from those outside—the second is perhaps that which controls their judgments all the time. But the literary excellence of the liturgy can be appreciated up to a point even when the Catholic faith is not accepted; at least we may expect it to be appreciated in so far as it is possible to concentrate upon the side of beauty, if we can persuade people to take it seriously at all."

It is no doubt true that holiness is possible for the individual without any visible repercussions in that vast sphere of human activity to which we refer when we speak of "art" in the broad sense of the word. Nevertheless such a state of things is surely abnormal. The vital connections between religion and culture have been the theme of Mr Christopher Dawson's work for many years past, and in his recent Gifford lectures he has shown us how the Liturgy was once the very soul of a culture. We must not, then, *acquiesce* in a state of affairs in which the Liturgy has ceased to form the mentality, and to be the natural expression, even of those social groups which have remained most staunchly

Catholic. When we look at things in this way, we may excusably feel a certain helplessness in face of the contemporary situation. But it may help us to keep our minds clear, to preserve some islands of firm ground in the great shifting sea of paganism which surrounds us. At least it shows that to bring our best critical powers to bear upon the language and all the art-forms of the Liturgy is not always to indulge in a mere 'aestheticism'.

On the Octave Day of Easter, *Dominica in Albis*, the catechumens, having laid aside their white garments, celebrated the holy mysteries for the first time as full-grown members of Christ's body; they had now completed their public profession of lifelong loyalty to their baptismal vows. This was a social and cultural event of the greatest importance (we are beginning to realize nowadays how much difference it makes when converts are gained, instructed and received into the Church not as isolated individuals but in groups). I have already referred to the Mass for this day, but it demands further notice. The Roman Station is at the Church of the fourteen-year-old martyr, St Pancras, the type of faithfulness and loyalty. The first words of the Mass, "Like new-born babes", introduce us with extraordinary vigour into the dominant thought: that faith is a *beginning*, a love-gift, precious and delectable (I am trying to catch the spirit of *Quasimodo* with these phrases), but nevertheless something as yet fresh and undeveloped, lively but not yet strong. We must be always looking forward, keeping the Paschal feast in our conduct and our lives (as the Collect says), giving our gifts exultingly (the Secret continues), because we have been given cause for such great joy, finding in the sacred mysteries (in the language of the Post-Communion) the healing of our souls now and for ever. And the Gospel (the incident of doubting Thomas) tells us that, although Christ leads us towards faith in him by visible signs, the gift of faith itself pierces the veil of the visible. The genuine lover of truth, the genuine philosopher, will hear Christ's voice in this Mass with a strange distinctness. *Sine dolo lac concupiscite.* St Peter's language, in a moving though minor key, echoes the awe-inspiring words which St John has preserved for us: "for this was I born, and for this came I into the world, that I should bear witness to the truth: he who is of the truth hears my voice".

"Hearing Christ's voice" is a *leit-motif* in these Eastertide Masses. A growing intimacy with him is insisted upon, not merely a moral imitation but a personal *knowledge*. For we are approaching Pentecost, when we celebrate the definite establishment of the society which is what it is precisely because it is the focus of this intimacy. The life of faith is to develop, as the Mass for the Second Sunday after Easter, Good Shepherd Sunday, seems to bring out. Again we have St Peter (in the Epistle) telling us in his practical way to follow in the footsteps of our Shepherd (a subject on which his thoughts must have dwelt continuously ever since Christ gave him his sheep to feed), and again it is St John who gives us the words of the Gospel, echoed so fittingly both in the Alleluia verse and in the Communion Antiphon: "I know my sheep and mine know me". Between the two the Offertory Antiphon, looking at it from the point of view of the sheep, drives home St Peter's lesson: *Deus, Deus meus, ad te de luce vigilo*. The psalm at the Introit was inevitably the thirty-second, the psalm of the Good Shepherd; this one, the sixty-second, is too much in the contemplative spirit of the season for us to regret the change-over.

You remember how St John rather bored some of his disciples by saying to them time and again: "Little children, love one another", and how he excused himself on the ground that really there was nothing else to say. Anyone who proposes to comment on the chants of these Paschal Masses is in a position rather like St John's. The Missal goes on saying *exsultate, jubilate* and so on, to the accompaniment of strings of *Alleluias*. But these chants are not meant to be *said*. When they are sung, you realize how exquisitely *varied* is the Church's joy. They reinforce (quite eerily) the variations upon the theme of the Easter victory which the texts of the Masses are executing. The general result is one of convincingness: that they are bursting with the Christian fact; it is altogether certain, and inexhaustible. Experts tell us that nobody really knows how the Gregorian chant was meant to be sung. Well, if the way in which some of these experts in fact sing it is only their guess, the result is an even greater wonder. Eric Gill describes somewhere how he became convinced of

God's existence by hearing the chant, a confession which has lifted eyebrows. I confess that I see nothing to disapprove of in such a conjunction.

The Third Sunday begins with the *Jubilate* psalm sixty-five, which is to be a sort of refrain for the next few weeks. We might be inclined to suppose that a somewhat sombre mood would be introduced into this Mass, since the Gospel contains our Lord's words to his disciples about his approaching departure. But his great point in this passage is that they ought *not* to be sad about it. It is just because he is going to the Father that no man shall take away their joy, for he is going to prepare a place for them. So far from regarding the Ascension as an event which should temper the excitement of Easter, the Church regards it as a stage in a continuous *crescendo* of that *sobria ebrietas*, sober drunkenness, for which she prays in the hymn for Lauds on Sundays. But the Masses of this time, though so far removed from anything like sombreness, are not therefore lacking in seriousness. We have a series of Epistles from St Peter and St James which insist on the implications of our redeemed state, the duty of aiming at perfection and the need for constant vigilance in the daily round. Concurrent with these Epistles is a series of Gospels taken from St John's sixteenth chapter in which our Lord's teaching leads us into the depths of his mystery, the ineffable union of the Three Divine Persons with one another and our union with them by their presence in our souls. The prayers on the Fourth Sunday are the despair of the modern translator. Cranmer's version of the collect in which we pray that "amid all the changes and chances of this mortal world our hearts may surely there be fixed where true joys are to be found" has so inevitable a rhythm that it is difficult to do anything else except produce a botching of it. But it has not the firmness and conciseness of the Latin: *ut inter mundanas varietates ibi nostra fixa sint corda, ubi vera sunt gaudia*. The Secret, rather freely translated, is as follows: "God, who have made us sharers in the one supreme divinity by this solemn exchange of gifts, this holy sacrifice, grant that as we know your truth we may pursue it and be worthy of it in our lives." The Gospel for the Fifth Sunday shows us what in particular we are to do. That our joy may be full we are to pray in the name of Jesus, that is to say we are to pray the Church's prayer, Christ's prayer, the prayer of the Liturgy.

Dom Parsch has some considerations to offer us on the Gospel of the Fifth Sunday which are worth stopping to ponder. "I came forth from the Father", our Lord here tells us, "and came into the world. Again I leave the world and go to the Father". Here, says Dom Parsch, we have the whole redemptive mystery, the double cycle of the Liturgical Year, Christmas and Easter. He goes on to point out that our Lord has said a little earlier in the same passage: "I have told you these things in parables. But the hour is coming when I shall speak to you no more in parables, but I shall speak to you openly of the Father." "The life of Christ", Dom Parsch also writes, "his miracles and his actions were the figures of his action in the Church and in souls. Our task is to study the life of our Lord and to see there the image of his action on ourselves. This gives us the key which will open to us the innermost meaning of Holy Scripture. We are not to concentrate exclusively upon the Gospel as a historical record; that is not the Liturgy's way. The Church does not intend to announce to us what is past but what is present. All the fullness of the Gospels belongs to the Church, and, in the Church, to us."

Of the Mass for the Feast of the Ascension I have only this to remark: that it is full of the thought on which the Fathers so often dwelt of *our* glorification through Christ's entrance into heaven with our human nature. We might perhaps call this feast the original feast of Christ the King. There is no occasion for saying more about this Mass because it is what we should expect it to be. But the Sunday following, the last before Pentecost, brings to some of us, perhaps, a surprise. The Introit is not one of those fanfares with which we have been regaled on the Sundays after Easter. It comes from the twenty-sixth psalm, and is a passionate, pleading appeal: *Quaesivi vultum tuum, vultum tuum, Domine, requiram ... ne avertas faciem tuam a me.* "Turn not your face from me"—it sounds like Lent. *Vultum tuum, vultum tuum, Domine*—the repetition is not sentimental (the ancient Liturgy is never that), but there is a depth of feeling which we cannot translate into English. For one thing *vultus* is not really "countenance", which is a fussy sort of word. It is one of the great Christian words which are both simple and profound. *O Jesu, tuum vultum, quem colimus occultum* ... And "face" is too thin a word. So we must pass on. The Collect deals more directly than is usual in the Liturgy with the secrets of the heart, praying that our wills may be devoted and our intentions sincere. St Peter's words about charity in the Epistle drive this home. The Secret asks that the sacrifice may give our minds the vigour (*vigorem*) of heavenly grace. What is the explanation of all this peculiar intensity and urgency? Why has the *crescendo* of thanksgiving died down? I suppose for the reason why a *crescendo* always does—because the moment before the final climax is always a breathless and critical one. We are at that point of eager anticipation when our joy is turned, not indeed to sorrow, but to a kind of anxiety. This may seem a fanciful explanation. But if we look at the rest of the Mass we shall have to admit at the least that there is in it a markedly subdued tone and that this is connected somehow with the proximity of Pentecost. "I shall not leave you orphans", the Alleluia verse begins, as if at the last moment there were some need to be reassured. In the Gospel our Lord promises us the Spirit of Truth and at the same time warns us of persecution; in the Communion antiphon we use his prayer that those whom he has kept safe while he was with them may be kept safe from evil now that he is leaving them. Undoubtedly there is a special mood in this Mass. And the longing which it expresses gains in significance when we remember that the Church is always looking to the future, to the final *parousia*. "Maranatha! Come, Lord Jesus."

At Pentecost, unless we have the Easter Sunday Mass in mind, we shall probably experience another surprise. For here again the *crescendo* ends not in a *fortissimo* but in restrained majesty. And again it proves to be a worthy climax. *Spiritus Domini replevit orbem terrarum*—"the Spirit of God has filled the whole world"; but "filled" does not do justice to *replevit*. The Gregorian chant emphasizes the strength of this language (the repetition of "R" is one reason for its effectiveness). In the Preface the note of ecstasy breaks out: *totus in orbe terrarum mundus exsultat*, but in general it is the feeling of awe that predominates, the profound sense of God's generosity which has embraced all nations, which has made his Church *Catholic*, and the reverence with which she contemplates his gift to her of himself. The coming of the tongues of fire, related in the Epistle and repeated in the Communion Antiphon, symbolizes both the Holy Spirit himself and the effect of his descent among men. Naturally we think of the Holy Spirit as the flame which darts out under the impact of two infinitely powerful forces, the self-bestowal of the Father upon the Son, and the self-surrender of the Son to the Father. The Gospels taken from St John have prepared us during the past weeks for the definitive revelation of the Divine Life. In to-day's Gospel we are told that the Son's message is not his, but the Father's; that they will take up their dwelling with us in our souls; that the Paraclete is to be sent in Christ's name to teach us all things. So, says our Lord, I leave you my peace; not as the world gives do I give to you. All true Trinitarian theology must spring from meditation upon these words. This is indeed the fulfilment of Easter. Without Easter, no Pentecost; just as without Christmas, no Epiphany. But just as we are not to regard our Lord's birth as an end in itself, so we are not to regard Easter as completing the circle of the Liturgical Year. It is rather the great turning-point. The time of full fruition is Pentecost.

To enter more fully into the significance of the feast for our own lives we must study some more of the texts in the Mass. They tell us that it is true charity, the charity which is rooted in the adoration of God, which is the attractive and unifying force, through which the dispersal of humanity, the disruptive force of sin, is to be overcome. The disciples were praying together when the sound from heaven heralded the coming of the Spirit. The Spirit came upon them and in the power of the Spirit those who had been strangers, inaccessible, became as their kinsmen. The barriers which the building of the tower of Babel had put up were thrown down. But this was only a beginning. In principle the Spirit has gone forth to the ends of the earth. But the Church still grows up and must still pray in every age for the Spirit. The magnificent sequence *Veni, Sancte Spiritus*, one of the very few Sequences retained by our Missal, is her prayer. The Offertory seems to enhance the atmosphere of awe and gratitude: "Confirm, O God, that which you have performed in us". These words from the sixty-seventh psalm, the psalm of the royal procession to Jerusalem, are wonderfully adapted to suggest what I would venture to call Christian reticence. Looking back over the whole course of the Christian mystery, we can find no words to describe what has happened except that it is what God has performed in us. And then the second verse of the Offertory-psalm, the Secret and the Post-Communion prayer speak volumes: "Kings shall offer to you gifts in your temple which is in Jerusalem ... Sanctify the gifts which we have offered and cleanse our hearts with the enlightenment of the Holy Spirit ... May it make them fruitful by the hidden sprinkling of its dew."

The subject of the Liturgy's reticence is worth pursuing. What I should wish to say has been said so effectively by Romano Guardini that I shall quote at some length from the English translation of his little book on the Spirit of the Liturgy. "There are certain feelings of surrender, certain aspects of interior candour which cannot be publicly proclaimed, at any rate in their entirety, without danger to spiritual modesty. The Liturgy has perfected a masterly instrument which has made it possible for us to express our inner life in all its fullness and depth, without divulging our secrets. *Secretum meum mihi.* We can pour out our hearts, and still feel that nothing has been dragged to light that should remain hidden."[1] Guardini has pointed out in the same paragraph that the Liturgy does, as he puts it, "awaken very profound and very tender emotions and impulses", but that it veils the secrets of the heart in imagery which is itself, although so rich, perfectly restrained. This comment applies exactly, I think, to the prayers which I have just quoted. In a later passage, Guardini makes a similar reflection upon liturgical actions in general, with special reference to the kiss of peace: "When it is performed according to the rubric," he observes, "it is a masterly manifestation of restrained and elevated social solidarity".

Two further passages are particularly worth recalling. The first is a warning which emerges from the point just made. "It is hardly necessary to point out what would be the infallible consequences of attempting to transmit the consciousness of their fellowship ... directly from one individual to another. The

[1] *The Spirit of the Liturgy*, Sheed and Ward, p. 22.

history of the sects teems with examples bearing on this point. For this reason the Liturgy sets strict bounds between individuals. Their union is moderated by a continually watchful sentiment of disparity and by reciprocal reverence. Their fellowship notwithstanding, the one individual can never force his way into the intimacy of the other, never influence the latter's prayers and actions, nor force upon the latter his own characteristics, feelings and perceptions. Their fellowship consists in community of intention, thought and language, in the direction of eyes and heart to the one aim ..."[1] The other passage is a footnote to the first words quoted above from Guardini: "The Liturgy here accomplishes on the spiritual plane what has been done on the temporal by the dignified forms of social intercourse, the outcome of the tradition created and handed down by sensitive people. This makes communal life possible for the individual ... he is in communication with his neighbours without being on that account swallowed up and lost among the crowd. In the same way the Liturgy preserves freedom of spiritual movement for the soul by means of a wonderful union of spontaneity and the finest erudition. It extolls *urbanitas* as the best antidote to barbarism, which triumphs when spontaneity and culture alike are no more." The Holy Father has warned us in the Encyclical *Mystici Corporis* against the dangers of a false mysticism which seeks to unite us with one another without first uniting us with Christ, the true Head.

It is taken for granted in the Missal that the Mass itself is the Christian Mystery in fully developed form, the Mystery, that is to say, which here incorporates us into itself. Although I do not propose to follow the course of the Liturgical Year beyond the climax of Pentecost, I should like to suggest in passing that the Feast of Corpus Christi, coming as a sort of comment on that climax, makes that presupposition explicit in a peculiarly felicitous way. But I shall say nothing of the famous Mass with St Thomas's prayers and sequence. And instead of making a hopeless attempt to select from the many Masses after Pentecost, in which the meaning of the Mystery is developed from many points of view, it seems better to pass them over entirely and to take the opportunity thus provided for a few words

[1] *Ibid.* pp. 48-9.

about the Masses for the Feasts of the Saints which occur
around Pentecost, since otherwise the Sanctoral will not receive
any mention at all.

The very existence of the Sanctoral, of a cycle of Saints'
feasts which operates on principles of its own, may give rise to
resentment. And it is perfectly true that the great cycle is at
present rather overlaid with these Feasts, which in some cases
have octaves, thereby switching us, so to speak, on to another
track for a whole week. The attempts of liturgical commentators
to claim for the total result a balanced and harmonious progress
of ideas, a successful interweaving of the lessons taught by these
Feasts with those taught by the particular liturgical season, cannot be considered altogether happy. Nevertheless there is a good
deal to be said along these lines for, say, the cluster of Saints
after Christmas and even for the intrusion of the Feast of the
Immaculate Conception into Advent. But the subject will not
be developed here. All that I propose to do is to draw attention
to a few of the Saints' Masses with a view to showing that, without them, our liturgical literature would be very greatly im-
poverished. Turning then, to the month of June, and making a
selection, we find on the second the Mass of the Roman
Martyrs Marcellinus, the priest, and Peter, the exorcist, whose
names occur in the Canon of the Mass. (Abbot Cabrol's book
The Year's Liturgy gives a handy account of them.[1] He tells us of
the discovery of their tomb in 1897 and of the inscription of
St Damasus, who was told the story of their beheading under
Diocletian by their executioner.) The Mass *Clamaverunt justi*
uses the thirty-third psalm for both the Introit and the Gradual,
and the chant is admirably suited to the theme of the freeing of
the just from their tribulations. In the Epistle St Paul compares
the suffering of the present time with future glory. In the Gospel
our Lord speaks of persecution and assures his future martyrs
that they will be safe in his hands. In fact all the parts of this
Mass, which have been nearly all taken over from the Common
Masses of Martyrs, fit in with one another in a most satisfying
way. On the 4th we have the Mass of St Francis Caracciolo, who
died in 1608 and founded the Congregation of Clerics Regular
Minor. It is very different in character. The air of high generality

[1] p. 242.

CL   H

which is common to the earlier Masses gives place to an attempt
to paint a particular picture by a rather mechanical assemblage
of texts. The prayers are cumbrous, and the Secret, addressed to
Jesus, makes no mention of the gifts. The Mass of St Boniface
on the 5th, although it does mention the gifts, is rather on the
same lines. If we pass on to the Feast of St Barnabas on the
11th, we find that the chants are common to other Feasts of
Apostles and that they are more subtly allusive and more dignified ("You will appoint them princes over all the earth" is the
beginning of the Offertory antiphon from the forty-fourth
psalm). And we shall find that it is the same with the other
Masses which draw upon the Commons, that for St Basil the
Great on the 14th which uses the Common of Doctors, *In
medio Ecclesiae aperuit os ejus;* that of St Juliana Falconieri on
the 19th which uses the Mass of Virgins, *Dilexisti,* taken largely
from the forty-fourth psalm, an essentially liturgical psalm, as
Abbot Cabrol calls it, "an epithalamium which sings of the
union between Christ and his Church";[1] that of St Paulinus on
the 22nd which uses the Common of Confessor Pontiffs with a
curiously impressive insistence upon David (*propter David
servum tuum ... memento Domine, David ... inveni David
servum meum*).

But it is particularly the Common Masses of the Martyrs
which are to be found during this month, and it would be a great
pity if we were ever to lose any of them. The Church's love for
her martyrs and the effects of it upon her Liturgy are very
fruitful subjects of study. Baptism was for the early Christians
a preparation for martyrdom (P. Daniélou's recent book on
Origen discusses this most interestingly). There are nine of
these Masses of Martyrs to be found at the end of the Missal, of
which the last two, *Protexisti* and *Sancti tui,* are for one Martyr
and many Martyrs respectively in Paschaltide. *Sancti tui,* occurs
in the Missal no less than six times in the first three weeks of
June for use when Easter has come late, so we may just glance
at it. The Introit is from the hundred and forty-fourth psalm,
which is unfortunately seldom used elsewhere in the Liturgy, as
Dom Parsch has pointed out. It describes the risen Christ surrounded by his witnesses. In the Epistle we have St Peter's

[1] *Ibid,* p. 228.

words about the trying of our faith which is far more precious than gold. In the Alleluia verse the exulting tones characteristic of the Easter Masses are combined with the peculiarly personal intensity of the text: *sicut odor balsami erunt ante te*. The Gospel is that of the vine and its branches from the fifteenth chapter of St John, for Christ is the king of Martyrs. And the Offertory and Communion Antiphons use the thirty-first and thirty-second psalms with absolute propriety to describe the joys of the just.

But it would be most misleading to suggest that the excellences of the Sanctoral are to be found only in the Commons. So it will be proper to end with a fine Mass which is proper to a Saint, and the obvious choice is that for the Nativity of St John the Baptist, which follows closely upon those just mentioned. It is true that the Offertory from the ninety-first psalm does occur elsewhere, but it is obviously St John's Offertory in a very special way. For he is the very type of the just man who shall flourish like the palm and to compare him with a cedar of Lebanon is eminently appropriate: indeed the combination of strength and grace which the comparison suggests characterizes the whole Mass. In the Introit from Isaias St John himself speaks: "From my mother's womb the Lord has called me by my name: and he has made my mouth like a sharp sword: he has covered me with the shelter of his hand and made me as his chosen arrow" (*posuit os meum ut gladium acutum ... quasi sagittam electam*: the chant exploits these sonorous phrases to the full). The Epistle sets the passage in the splendour of its full context. The Gradual "before I formed you in the womb, I knew you" is taken from Jeremias to show us that the Precursor is foreshadowed by this prophet too as well as by Isaias. The Alleluia verse, a chant of delightful simplicity, introduces the Gospel from St Luke about the marvels which attended the birth: *Tu puer propheta altissimi vocaberis*. This is repeated by the Communion antiphon. The Secret is a little long but its length is more than justified: "We heap your altars, O Lord, with our gifts, celebrating with due honour the birth of him who both prophesied (*cecinit*—the classical word) that the saviour of the world would come and proclaimed him as present, Jesus Christ, your Son, our Lord who lives and reigns ..." (the usual conclusion follows). The Post-Communion prayer matches it: "May your Church, O God, gain joy at the birth of Blessed John Baptist, through whom she has known the author of her own rebirth, your Son our Lord ..."

It is fitting that we should end with this Feast for it takes us back to the beginning. June 24th corresponds to the winter equinox, and the birth of St John, the summer Christmas, was once celebrated as solemnly as Christmas itself. The intense devotion of the early Church and of the first monks to St John the Baptist, the only saint save our Lady whose birth was sanctified and therefore commemorated by the Liturgy, is a fact which deserves our closest consideration. And the Collect of the Mass may sum up for us that attitude of mind which the whole Liturgical Year seeks to form in us:[1] "O God, who has made this day venerable for us by the birth of the Blessed John, grant to your peoples the grace of spiritual joys and direct the minds of all the faithful [there is a reference here to the Precursor's function] into the way of eternal salvation."

[1] P. Daniélou's *Bible et Liturgie*, the latest volume of the Lex Orandi series (*Les Editions du Cerf*), is of the greatest value as showing the dependence of liturgical symbolism on the Old Testament and the significance of the Liturgical Year as a whole for Christians of the early centuries.

IX

SINGING THE MASS AND OTHER
MODERN PROBLEMS

YOU MAY REMEMBER THAT SOME OF THE OBJECTIONS TO liturgical worship which we considered at the beginning were put off for further treatment at a later stage. What they amounted to was, briefly, this: that our practice is so far removed from our theory that we cannot expect the theory to be taken very seriously. Congregations often seem to take no part in what is going on and to take no interest in it. How, indeed, should they, in view of the meaninglessness of most of it? In this chapter I propose to consider what the answer should be.

First we must appreciate the extent of the difficulty. In beginning my remarks about the text of the Mass I suggested that we should consider ourselves as taking part in a Dialogue Mass so that we might not be so much distracted by the present problem. The time has now come to face it. We may begin by observing that Dialogue Mass is confined to certain parts of the world, and that it is not viewed with complacency by ecclesiastical authority. The position, as shown from the Holy Father's words in *Mediator*, is that Dialogue Mass is viewed as a makeshift or at best as something which falls something far short of the ideal. Manifestly it does fall short, for the ideal is surely the High Mass of the Roman Rite. Dialogue Mass is a most valuable and necessary stage on the way to a full participation of the congregation in celebrating Mass. We are entitled to *hope*, I think, that it may become the norm for Low Mass. But the norm of the Mass, absolutely speaking, is the Mass sung partly by the priest, partly by a choir and partly by the congregation, and accompanied with all the ceremonial which the rubrics prescribe.

In speaking of the High Mass of the Roman rite as the "ideal" and the "norm", I have been referring, obviously, only to those parts of the world where the Roman rite is at present in use; I do not wish to be understood as implying that the Roman rite must be taken with them by missionaries wherever they go.[1] And by speaking of the "ideal" I do not mean to exclude the possibility of other rites growing up even in places which have used the Roman rite from the earliest times; if our present civilization is about to disappear, it will perhaps be replaced by another of a very different kind which will develop a very different liturgical style—this is a state of affairs which we find it difficult to envisage, no doubt, but, since there is nothing in the nature of things (or, more precisely, in the nature of the Church) to prevent it, the possibility, I suggest, cannot be excluded. By an "ideal", then, I mean the end to which our present endeavours should be directed, the only goal at which we can at present aim. It follows, if what I have so far said is true, that the Dialogue Mass should be considered as a means to this end. But it does not follow that we should regard the abolition of all Low Masses as an aim; indeed if we did we should be disobeying the Holy See. There will always be circumstances in which Low Mass is the only sort of Mass that can be celebrated. What is meant by saying that High Mass is the norm is simply that it is the *best* thing, the standard to which we should conform so far as possible.

If it be objected that the part played by the congregation is too restricted in the Roman High Mass and that in any case the distinction which I have made between the congregation and the choir is undesirable, my reply would be I am concerned with *practical* ideals: the opinion which I have expressed (with a full realization that it is only an opinion and a highly controversial one) is based on three suppositions: first, that the possibilities of the Roman rite have not been sufficiently explored in our time for us to pass an adverse judgment on them, to treat lightly the heritage which has been bequeathed to us, second, that the singing of the plainchant Propers in their entirety is impossible for most congregations, and third, that to aim at excluding these Propers from our churches, even if we except those of the monasteries, is to throw away an important part of this heritage without sufficient reason. Hence the retention of a

[1] P. Daniélou's book *The Salvation of the Nations* may be usefully consulted on this.

choir. A time may come when the Gregorian chant so far ceases to have any meaning for us that there is no point in trying to retain any of it—I do not think that it is within measurable distance. Moreover, the Holy See has continued to advocate in the strongest terms the restoration of the Gregorian chant. It is not always realized that Pope Pius X's famous words in his *Moto proprio* of 1903, "the faithful assemble to gain this [Christian] spirit from its primary and indispensable source", are followed by the clause "which is the active participation in the most holy Mysteries and in the public and solemn prayer of the Church". The source is not just the Liturgy, but participation in the Liturgy and (the whole context shows) that implies to this end we must all aim at *singing* the Mass. But it is often impracticable to insist from the outset on the singing of the plainchant (even of the Ordinary) by the congregation. The great thing, for a start, is that it should *sing*, in a dignified manner, that is; and here I beg leave to refer to the very simple setting of the Ordinary by Dom Gregory Murray, Monk of Downside, *A People's Mass*, which has been gaining some notable successes not only in England but at Lourdes. (In his booklet *The Choral Chants of the Mass*, the composer argues that the Masses of the Kyriale were never meant for congregational use.) The German *Singmesse* too, with its liturgical hymns, is of great value provided that it is considered to be a temporary expedient, and the general aim of uniting priest and people in the *same* prayer is not forgotten. The question of vernacular renderings of the Roman rite I propose to regard as a separate one; I shall say something about it later.

The extent of the difficulty should now be clear: we are a very long way from that healthy participation of the laity in High Mass which I have suggested as the ideal. It is true that we can hardly imagine circumstances in which a High Mass would be a regular occurrence in a country village. There a sung Mass is the most that can be expected. But how many churches there are in which Mass is an almost completely silent affair except when the priest gets into the pulpit! Unless we have experienced it, we may have some difficulty in realizing the sense of shock and disappointment with which a non-Catholic sometimes encounters the Mass for the first time. The priest, while he is at the altar, seems so often to give no sign of wishing to establish intelligible contact with the congregation. Admittedly they would not understand, for the most part, the Latin text; but surely they are supposed to be following it in their own way— and, in fact, nobody is getting a chance to follow it at all. Some- times the explanation is that the priest is accustomed to saying Mass in a church where there is more than one altar in use at a time (in that case the rubrics direct him not to disturb another celebrant). But the plain fact is that the rubrics which regulate the tone which the priest should use are very widely ignored. This is a grave abuse, and there is no sense in trying to cover it up. I do not suggest that the abuse is deliberate. In fact it is sometimes thought to be "devotional" to say Mass inaudibly! In the case of a sung or High Mass the same sort of trouble is constantly arising. The congregation is listening to a musical performance in which it is taking little or no part and with which it does not appear to be in any way concerned. The same may be true of the ceremonies. The congregation will alter its posture from time to time in a patient sort of way, but it does not seem to be deriving any benefit from the actions which are being performed on the sanctuary. The answer which has to be given to all this is, I shall suggest, that despite these appear- ances the first half of this century has witnessed a great awaken- ing. The finest minds in the Catholic Church are keenly aware of our needs in regard to the Liturgy. If we can show our ques- tioner something of what has been done already and what may be expected to happen in the near future, we shall have gone a long way towards meeting his difficulty.

That is a topic on which I shall add a few details shortly. Here it seems necessary to pause for a short while to say something about the ceremonies and prayers special to High Mass, which have received so far only some incidental mentions. There are a number of further anomalies to consider. Let us suppose that we are assisting at the conventional form of High Mass in England. The singing of the Introit, instead of accompanying the procession to the altar, is sung by a choir while the prayers are being said at the foot of the altar. What is the congregation supposed to be doing at this time? With luck we shall all take part in singing the *Kyrie Eleison* and the *Gloria*, and we shall hear the prayers and the Epistle, although perhaps with difficulty, because the sacred ministers are facing away from us. Nevertheless this is an immense improvement on Low Mass. We can then take our choice between trying to get something out of the choir's efforts with the Gradual and the Alleluia or following the ceremonial leading to the Gospel procession, before which the celebrant says the Gospel to himself. The Gospel is sung facing the north wall of the church, which is odd but need not make it hard to hear. Probably the Creed is the best piece of congregational singing. But at the Offertory not only have we practically nothing in particular to do ourselves but in all probability we are prevented from following the prayers (those for the blessing of the incense are well worth following) and even from attending to the ceremony of incensing (which can be a very great help to recollection) by musical items of various kinds supplied by the organist, with or without the choir, when they have disposed of the Offertory Antiphon. This is likely to go on up to and through the Secret prayers and may even hold up the celebrant when he is ready to sing *Dominus vobiscum*. After the Preface there might appear to be something in the nature of a plot to prevent the congregation from following the Canon. If the *Missa de Angelis* is sung (as it commonly is) with its rather late and florid *Sanctus*, and if the celebrant gets off the mark quickly (as he commonly does), the end of the singing may coincide with the bell at *Quam oblationem*. And the *Benedictus* is reserved for singing after the Consecration, followed as a rule by more improvisations at the organ. However, the disciplined movements of the deacon and sub-deacon should help us to realize what is going on (although the sub-deacon's use of the humeral veil cannot mean very much to us), and we can join in the great *Amen*, and the responses which follow.

The fact that the *Agnus Dei* is sung during the prayers before Communion will not often matter because usually the priest communicates alone. And this introduces the important topic of Communion at Sung or High Mass. It has been much discussed of late, and I would merely repeat the points that a Sung Mass need not take much longer than a Low Mass, so that there is really no great difficulty in having it before breakfast, and that in any case permission for Mass at other times of the day (accompanied by no exacting regulations about fasting) is being obtained with increasing facility, so that the difficulty can be done away with altogether. The rest of the Mass we can participate in pretty well. We have not exchanged the kiss of peace, but we have seen the ministers doing so. We have time to attend to the Post-Communion prayers. The singing of the *Ite Missa est* may emphasize the incongruity of this announcement when there is perhaps a prayer for the King to be sung as well as the usual additions. But, by and large, we have taken part in a ceremony which works, or at least can work.

What I wish to underline now is the determination not merely of liturgical groups but of the Church's rulers that it should work much better. And for the purpose I would refer you to a book by the well-known American Jesuit, Fr Ellard, *The Mass of the Future*. You will find in this book a very complete answer to the general difficulty with which we are grappling: that the Liturgy is "fossilized", a dead thing, out of contact with the lives of ordinary people. The answer is that it has been on the move for some time past.

It is not easy to find one's way about in Fr Ellard's book, which runs to over 350 large pages. The chapter headings (for example, "Augustine's 'Whole Priest' Still on Duty" and "Regrouping the Fuselage Fixtures") will not be very informative, at least to Europeans. And the little Latin headings to the paragraphs, although they do in fact refer to their contents in some fashion, are hardly less baffling. But the main structure of the book is clear. The first two parts form a history of the Mass-liturgy up to the present time with special reference to the great reforms of Pius X, and the book takes its name from the third part, a few passages from which I shall put before you. In these Fr Ellard gives rein to his imagination and paints a picture of the liturgical development which he anticipates in the years to come. They are, he argues, the logical consequences of the developments which have taken place in the recent past. Before referring to any of them I would point out that the book was published after the appearance of *Mediator*, to which it frequently refers, and has received the *imprimatur* of the Archbishop of Milwaukee, although a note is added to warn us that this does not commit anyone besides the author to the opinions which it expresses. The most notable perhaps of these suggestions is that "certain parts of the Mass be given the same bilingual freedom that the new rituals have for some time enjoyed ... the celebrant is to enjoy the option, as he may judge the greater good may be achieved, of using the customary Latin or an authorized vernacular rendition."[1] No change in the text of the Canon or in the rubrics affecting the Canon is envisaged. A further suggestion is that "if the united hierarchy of a nation (or language group) ask for it, the Holy See would be pleased to sanction and embody new musical arrangements for the 'hymned portions' of the vernacular in any of the proposed editions." Fr Ellard notes that the Encyclical *Mediator* must be understood as inveighing only against the *unauthorized* use of the vernacular.

He goes on to describe the contents of an imaginary new Missal. It contains a revision of the calendar. Easter is always to fall on the first Sunday of April. The Sunday Mass is not to be extruded from its position except when one of a carefully limited list of feasts coincides with it. The Sanctoral is to be simplified and the rubrics clarified. Some changes in the allotment of Gospel passages for Sundays is contemplated. The Epistle and Gospel are to be read or sung facing the people[2] (these are parts of the Mass where the vernacular is to be allowed). The celebrant need no longer read the Epistle and Gospel to himself at High Mass. The *Benedictus* may be sung before the Consecration. During the Communion, instead of after it, the Antiphon may be sung, together with its psalm, as a refrain. So also with the Offertory verse (it has already been declared licit to sing the Introit as a processional chant). At the end of the Canon the chalice is to be raised to the height of the eyes for the "Little Elevation" and a handbell rung. The priest should pause after the great *Amen* before beginning the *Pater Noster*, in which the congregation may join. The *Confiteor* before the people's Communion may be omitted. The *Ite Missa est* is to be postponed until after the Last Gospel. At Sung Masses the faithful should adopt the same positions as the ministers, and they should stand at Low Mass not only for the

[1] p. 251.
[2] This is, in fact, already permissible for the Epistle according to the *Caerimoniale Episcoporum*.

Gospel and Creed but also for the Introit, Preface and *Sanctus*, *Pater Noster* and *Agnus Dei*, and for the prayers of the Proper (not apparently for the Offertory).[1]

Then comes the chapter called "Regrouping the Fuselage Fixtures", which proves to be about the altar. It is pointed out that episcopal sanction can be gained for a free-standing altar (indeed the rubrics presuppose that it should be of that kind) so placed that it can be seen by the people, and a cruciform church with a two-faced central altar is recommended, an altar, that is, at which Mass can be said either facing towards the people or away from them. We then learn more about the proposed liturgical hymns. "A series of matched hymns" is recommended "giving the Proper in dignified hymn form, in seasonal melodies". The proposal is developed as follows. "For each pattern, two simple and worthy choral melodies are to be selected, one to serve for both Introit and Gradual hymn, the other to supply the Offertory and Communion hymns. The same melodies will be used Sunday after Sunday for that period of the Church Year, but the books provide new 'words' for each Sunday's Mass hymns. In a year or two the whole body of the faithful will know the melodies all by heart ..."[2] Fr Ellard also remarks that the bilingual Missal should be provided with plainsong in English.[3]

We must pass over what he has to say in his concluding chapter about reviving the Offertory procession, about a proposed "Guild Missal", containing an astonishing number of special Masses for vocational groups and about what he calls "convention celebration" or synchronized Masses at Congresses. There is more than enough to think about already. It will be obvious that many of the recommendations which I have been listing deserve the warmest welcome, that they would remove in principle the anomalies to which I have referred and that they might seem to herald the beginning of a great liturgical era. But there are several points on which a difference of opinion may be allowed. There is perhaps some danger that in our desire to bring congregations to life—and there should be no question about the urgency of this: there is no time to waste— some danger that we throw overboard too much and that we

[1] pp. 260-64.   [2] p. 277.   [3] p. 276.

may take on fresh burdens which we shall later regret. For example, an indiscriminate adoption of the "liturgical hymn" would militate against the restoration of the Gregorian chant for the Proper of the Mass, which I have ventured to suggest should remain, for the present at least, as something to be worked for whenever possible. In the same way it seems to me that we should continue to hope that some congregations, which have been induced to sing for the first time, let us say by the simplicity of some setting of the Ordinary like Dom Murray's, may come in time to learn the simpler plainchant versions of the Ordinary and to value the singing of the Gregorian Proper by the choir. Perhaps, even, they might be absorbed by the choir in gradually increasing numbers. And here a musical question arises on which I am not myself competent to speak but on which I should like to put before you Dom Murray's opinion. It concerns the singing of plainsong with the liturgical text translated into the vernacular, a proposal which Fr Ellard welcomes in his 29th chapter. He refers to the Anglican plainsong service-books and in particular to John Merbecke's adaptations in 1550 and the 19th century adaptations of Merbecke. In the bibliography at the end of the chapter he mentions Dom Murray's article in *The Downside Review* for April 1947, "Plainsong and a Vernacular Liturgy", but he does not discuss it in the text. In this article Dom Murray points out that Merbecke produced a new sort of music "a music that really suits the English language". It is something quite different from St Gregory's liturgical music, and Dom Murray concludes that "to attempt to marry it [St Gregory's music] to an English vernacular liturgy would be sheer vandalism, the desecration of a precious relic of our Catholic past".

Having said so much I ought to indicate, if only in a rough sort of way, the grounds for Dom Murray's conclusion. He maintains that plainsong and English cannot combine "for reasons which are intimately bound up with the nature of the two things". In plainsong the verbal accent is independent of the melodic rhythm and comes as a rule on the up-beat. It is a different sort of verbal accent from the English one, something much lighter. An English accent, which is normally long and heavy, comes on the down-beat. Dom Murray then adds a few illustrations of the way in which an English phrase is distorted by being adapted to plainsong. Moreover, in ecclesiastical Latin every accent is followed by one or two unaccented syllables. There is a certain "flow". Ét in térra páx homínibús (to take one of Dom Murray's examples)—how can music which is fitted to these words fit "and on eárth peáce to mén of good wíll"? Merbecke, then, "realized that English and genuine plainsong cannot combine without sacrificing either correct English accentuation or correct plainsong rhythm". Some may feel that the productions of the Plainsong and Mediaeval Music Society are evidence in a contrary sense. I have not wished to dogmatize about this issue, but only to put certain considerations before you.

Other points on which I feel uneasiness are the proposed changes in the Sunday Gospels, for the third and fourth Sundays after Easter are marked for change in this respect and this seems a pity, and the vigorous burgeoning of liturgical compositions which seems to be recommended. I doubt whether there is at the moment a sufficient literary and liturgical competence among us for all this composing of Masses (I have in mind here chiefly composition in Latin, for there does not seem to be much appreciation of the specific character of *Christian* Latin; some recent productions have evolved a tasteless hybrid which is neither Christian nor Ciceronian.) But I must mention these things, important though they are, only to dismiss them, because I must not stave off any longer the fundamental question: Is the Liturgy of the future to be in Latin at all? When we began to consider the liturgical year I threw out a hint that I did not propose to adopt an extreme position either way by remarking that if the Catholic schools could provide anything deserving the name of Catholic education, the arguments for a vernacular *Ordinary* would be considerably weakened. And I abstained from any further expression of opinion. Now I find myself obliged to say something further, and, speaking like Milton's Adam (according to Sir Walter Raleigh) "out of the depths of my inexperience" (parochial problems being rather unfamiliar to me) I must confess that in recent years a rooted objection on my part to vernacular Liturgy in any form has been slowly undermined by what has seemed to be the logic of facts. In

England, at any rate, there is the most pressing need to give the congregation the opportunity to take their proper part in the liturgical action at Mass, and I do not believe that we shall get them to do it, in some areas at least, except by the liturgical use of their own language. Nevertheless I regard this as a necessity which brings with it serious drawbacks and dangers, not on the ground that the Liturgy is in itself incompatible with the vernacular (which a moment's thought should show to be an absurd suggestion, whether viewed historically or in the abstract), but because we are not in a fit state to evolve a new Liturgy and may be running the risk of damaging and eventually even destroying our old one. This may be (I hope it is) exaggerated language. But in any case a translation of the Roman Mass into English would not of itself solve our problems. Even if it were backed up with intensive liturgical preaching (which is absolutely indispensable on any plan), it would be a very awkward affair for public use, often becoming either a stilted or a garbled version which in places at least might be almost as difficult to explain as the Latin. And there is another all-important consideration. Any liturgical culture must be a Biblical culture. A re-education of the faithful in the Bible must accompany liturgical preaching if our efforts are to produce solid and lasting results.

The value of the existing Latin Liturgy does not lie in the uniformity which it gives to the worship of the Roman rite. And to suggest that the *Catholica* enjoys this measure of uniformity by reason of its inner constitution instead of as a result of historical accidents would be a gross error. Uniformity of faith has no necessary connection with uniformity of language. But these historical accidents are of the utmost importance. *In fact* the Latin of the Church has been the liturgical expression of her life in the past, and our spiritual roots may be embedded in it far more deeply than we realize. That, I believe, is the reason why we should proceed with the utmost caution—not for the benefit of those travelling abroad who find themselves at home in Church, but for the benefit of the millions who have remained at home, in other words for the glory of God—for there is another bad argument against a vernacular Liturgy according to which the Liturgy is for the glory of God and *not* for the benefit of the people.

But the benefit of the people does seem to demand a compromise in the present situation. It is true, in general, that we must bring the people up to the level of the Liturgy and not bring it down to their level. Nevertheless we must make it easier for them if they are to keep in touch with it to-day. I conclude that it is not enough to supply them with explanatory leaflets with the Mass in Latin and English. It is excellent so far as it goes, but liturgical hymns in the vernacular are also needed, for children's Masses certainly, and in many other cases. Perhaps in some places and for some time the whole Mass may have to be in the vernacular up to the Gospel or even to the Preface.[1] I am deliberately envisaging only short-term policies. They are inevitably experimental, untidy and provisional. The fact is that we cannot see into the future with any degree of clearness. We cannot, I think, make plans for achieving the absolute ideal of a common prayer, a prayer in which priest and people pray together in the same language. All we can do is to bring them more and more closely together in the existing framework of the traditional rites. And only experience can teach us how best to do it. One thing is perfectly clear: that the great mass of the people is woefully ignorant of the significance of the Liturgy and of their part in it. But the wonderful results of the liturgical apostolate in our time, although its influence is still a very limited one, show what we may hope for in the future. These results should be studied in detail, for example in the pages of such liturgical periodicals as *La Maison Dieu* in France, *Orate Fratres* in America and *Liturgy* in England.

The people's participation in the Liturgy has been promoted in Germany with impressive results. Yet one of the great leaders of German thought has written words which might seem to tell against much that I have said on this subject. Romano Guardini considers that "the claim that the Liturgy should be taken as the exclusive pattern of devotional practice in common can never be upheld. To do so would be to confess complete ignorance of the spiritual requirements of the greater part of the faithful. The forms of popular piety should exist side by

[1] The first German Liturgical Congress, held in Frankfurt in June 1950, petitioned the German bishops (some of whom were present) to submit to the Holy See a request for authorization of the rendering of the Epistle and Gospel in the vernacular at Mass.

side with those of the Liturgy, and should constitute themselves
according to the varying requirements of historical, social and
local conditions. There could be no greater mistake than that of
discarding the valuable elements in the spiritual life of the
people for the sake of the Liturgy, or than the desire of assimi-
lating them to it."[1] I have felt obliged to put this passage before
you before I end this lecture because it suggests an important
point of view which must be carefully assessed. The real difference of opinion, as I see it, between this point of view and that
which I have urged does not concern the desirability of popular
devotions, in the sense of devotions which are special to time and
place; there is no good reason for disputing about that. It bears
upon the nature of the Liturgy. The Liturgy, it is true, deals
with the universal needs of mankind. It is necessarily traditional
and conservative.[2] But at the same time it is subject, like all living
things, to the law of gradual evolution, and a clearcut distinction between a changeless Liturgy and changing popular devotions seems to me unsatisfactory.[3] The Liturgy, I would say, is of
its nature *the* popular devotion.

[1] *The Spirit of the Liturgy*, pp. 7-8.
[2] Dom Beaudouin's explanation of the deacon's singing the Gospel to the wall
(*apud* Crogaert, *op. cit.*, I, p. 567) is a startling illustration of the abuse of con-
servatism: it seems that, when the churches were orientated, the rubric directing
the deacon to turn *to the north*, that is (before orientation) *away from the wall*,
was still literally interpreted.
[3] P. Bouyer's entertaining article on the present state of liturgical things in
France published in *Dieu Vivant* 19 is of special interest in this connection.
Cf. P. Congar's *Vraie et Fausse Reforme dans l'Eglise* in the collection "Unam
Sanctam" (Les Editions du Cerf) esp. pp. 50 f)

X

THE DIVINE OFFICE

ALAY PERSON WHO "SAYS THE OFFICE" IS A RARITY IN England, and is even regarded sometimes by those who ought to know better as a freak. In France, a few years ago, the Editor of *La Vie Spirituelle* in reply to his appeal for information from the laity about their use of the Office received over a hundred replies. The results of his enquiry are to be found in *La Vie Spirituelle* for January 1947, an issue devoted to the general subject of the Divine Office on which I shall draw very largely in what follows. It seems safe to say that where there is a true understanding of the Mass and a real participation in it a desire for participation in the Divine Office regularly occurs. For the Divine Office is the Church's praise spreading out from its centre, the Mass, over the rest of the day. Properly understood, it is essentially the sanctification of *time*, the drawing of particular periods between the celebration of one day's Mass and the next into the orbit, as it were, of the Eucharist. Nowadays it is commonly considered to be a monastic affair which is also imposed—and, it is sometimes said, unreasonably imposed—upon busy diocesan clergy who thus find themselves faced with a heavy hour's labour when they have at last disposed of more pressing duties and are ready for bed. To understand the present condition of the Divine Office we must have before us a brief sketch of its historical development.

The core of the Divine Office, the Psalter, is a legacy from the Old Testament. There might seem to be no point in making so banal a statement, were it not for what it might suggest to the unwary, that the Psalter is outdated; it is precisely this suggestion which must be completely discredited before any understanding of the Divine Office is possible. A legacy as such is a link between one generation and another, a sign of kinship and unity, a token of affection and a means of livelihood. It is only by accident that it is an embarrassment. To put this in another way, Christianity is a historical religion in the special sense that it is a way of life based on a doctrine of cosmic development.

This development is rooted in the Old Testament and comes to fruition in the New, with the Psalter acting as a sort of *vinculum substantiale* or vital link. The Psalter, that is to say, is both a condensation of the history of God's chosen people and a prefiguration of the new Israel. It is the great prophecy of the Incarnate Son, the great prayer of the Incarnate Son in his earthly life and the great preservative of the life of the Incarnate Son in his Mystical Body. It is no wonder that the first Christians were devoted to the psalms.

The first that we hear of their liturgical worship is that they "persevered in the doctrine of the Apostles, in the communication of the breaking of bread and in prayers" (Acts II. 42). And we have been reminded recently by P. Daniélou (*La Maison Dieu*, 21, p. 40 f.) that the *psalms* were not used as *prayers* until later. The hymns and canticles mentioned by St Paul (Eph. v. 19) were the prayers; the psalms came rather under the heading of doctrine: it was not only tremendously exciting to discover how the prophecies had been fulfilled ("were not our hearts burning within us as he spoke to us in the way?") but most enlightening—the psalms helped the first Christians, as they should help us, to know Christ better, to penetrate the sense of his own teaching. The Holy Spirit did not merely inspire the psalmist and then leave Holy Writ, so to speak, inanimate; he still acts in it and so reveals to us Christ's mystery.

But the early Christians did not use the psalms only in their new liturgical assembly, the Saturday vigil before the Sunday Eucharist at the hour of the Resurrection. They also continued to observe the Jewish hours of prayer. Terce, Sext and None are mentioned in the Acts, and there were also the great evening and morning prayers, the ancestors of the Christian Mattins (which was originally one with Lauds) and Vespers. Not only the Psalter, then, but the very structure of the Divine Office is a legacy from the Old Testament. It is a characteristic of the people of God in all ages that they should pray to God as a people at stated times and in a stated manner.

Here it will be convenient to quote from P. Henry's fine article in the issue of *La Vie Spirituelle* already mentioned, "Principes pour une meilleure intelligence de l'office", to which

I am greatly indebted throughout this chapter. He has just been speaking of the great weekly vigil, of Mattins, or rather, as he puts it, morning Lauds, and of the prayer at the close of day. "In the fourth and fifth centuries", he writes, "the churches had often adopted these three offices. They were full liturgical assemblies at which the faithful not only listened but actively assisted, answering the priest's prayers with the *Amen* and concluding the litanies given out by the deacons with *oramus te, miserere, Kyrie eleison*, and replying to the singing of the psalms with a 'response' or an 'antiphon' ".

The further developments of the Divine Office are of monastic origin. In the monasteries traditional customs became codified and fixed in a system of ordinances, and the principle of canonicity was then adopted by the clergy at large. Thus St Benedict found a developed Roman Liturgy to hand which became a basis for his own liturgical legislation. The monastic Mattins had already been put back in most places to before the dawn, in accordance with the advice of 3rd century preachers who had pointed out that it was unnecessary to remain asleep for the whole night (especially in winter when there might be as much as ten hours of darkness). A result of this was that Lauds became a separate function from Mattins. Cassian tells us that some lazy Syrian monks returned after Mattins to bed where they remained until the hour of Terce. So, to prevent this happening, Lauds was fixed for the hour of dawn, the traditional time for the morning prayer. Terce, Sext and None had also gained canonical status in the monasteries, recalling the monks to their prayers at about nine in the morning, at midday and in the early afternoon. Here again I cannot resist quoting P. Henry: "But sometimes the monks were not obliged to return to the church; a signal was given, and each in the midst of his occupations broke off to pray to the Lord. Doesn't that make us think of the Muezzins of Islam announcing the hour of prayer from the tops of the minarets? Nothing seems more useful for an understanding of our 'little hours' than to compare them with the present practice of the Mussulmans." It is a great joy to discover lay persons in some parts of the world reciting the "little hours" in the underground railway or on their way from their business to their lunch.

But the great hours of the Church's praise are the morning and evening prayers of Lauds and Vespers. These take less than a quarter of an hour to recite with decent reverence, and their general adoption, by the educated laity at least, is something which one can hardly advocate too strongly. This was urged very eloquently a few years ago by Edward Watkin in his book *Praise of Glory*.[1] I shall refer again to this book when I speak more particularly of the texts of the hours, but I should like to quote at this point his final footnote: "If there were sufficient demand for it a book containing Lauds and Vespers in Latin and English with full instructions for its use would no doubt soon be provided by a Catholic publisher. Already I see it in my mind's eye, Morning and Evening Praise, that is Lauds and Vespers, to be followed by another volume, Morning and Night Prayer, Prime and Compline. Those who cannot learn enough Church Latin, which after all is not the difficult Latin of Cicero, might well learn the general sense of the Latin text by constant use of the translation on an opposite page, until they could say the actual words employed by the Church and hallowed by the lips of generations of saints, understanding the sense of it from their knowledge of the English."

Something must now be said about Prime and Compline. Prime does not make its appearance until the beginning of the 6th century, and we do not find it as a daily prayer until the time of St Benedict, who established it as the prayer to be used before beginning the day's work. Compline too (the prayer for bedtime) was a relatively late arrival, taken over by St Benedict's Rule, which did not consolidate its position until the 8th or 9th century. Prime and Compline are, I need hardly say, admirable morning and evening prayers, but it is difficult not to wish that their popularization in modern times was based upon a popularization of Lauds and Vespers instead of substituting for it. I am not suggesting it as an objection that they are of purely monastic origin. But it is worth bearing in mind that Lauds and Vespers are of age-long popular origin. They are also of greater liturgical richness.

In the early Middle Ages the spread of the Benedictine monasteries led to the diffusion of the Roman Office throughout

[1] Sheed and Ward, 1943.

Europe, so that in the 11th century, through the efforts of Pope Gregory VII in particular, there was something approaching a common observance in the Western Church. But the period which followed was one of great liturgical confusion. The combining of the Psalter with the many other office books (the antiphoner, the hymnal and so forth) into a single portable volume was accompanied by a ruthless cutting down of the lessons and the antiphons. The chant was not favoured by many of the new Orders which were springing up, and the age of the Breviary was born. At the same time there was a burgeoning of new feasts, and of lessons of a pietistic and legendary nature. It was a time of liturgical license, and the ancient Liturgical Year seemed likely to disintegrate altogether.

The first attempt at a reformed Breviary adopted the existing distinction between the choir Office and the Office as said "privately". It might seem that there is something to be said for this, and in our own day the distinction is being recommended by high authorities. But it is contrary to the ancient traditions, and on that ground it was rejected by the Tridentine reformers. The Breviary of St Pius V was imposed on all clerics in 1568, only those churches and religious Orders being exempted which had used their own form of the Office for upwards of 200 years. Since that time little of great moment has been done by way of reform. St Pius V had, if I may so put it, stopped the rot, and his work has been followed up by some further improvements in the lessons and some further checks to the encroachments of new feasts upon the ancient "temporal". But the decree approving the present edition (1914) of the Breviary observes, as P. Henry points out, that there is still more improvement to be desired. The recently published revision of the Psalter is one attempt in this direction, but the texts of many lessons and hymns are in a state which is far from satisfactory. The calendar is still to some extent disorganized. And there are many minor anomalies.

Those who wish to become acquainted with the Breviary must be prepared, therefore, for some irritations and disappointments. But if they have gained from the Missal the true spirit of the Liturgy they will find ample compensation for these drawbacks. The greatest compensation of all is precisely the realization that this is the Church's Liturgy, the praise which the Church offers *officially* to God. Its arrangements may sometimes show the marks of human weakness, but the thing itself, this combination of the Old and New Testaments, with the Psalter at the heart of it and the patristic homilies commenting on it, with its ancient hymns and its collects which are (normally) the collects for the Mass of the day, all this is set before us by the Church as her daily prayer, and therefore as our daily prayer in so far as we can make it so. We cannot doubt that the substance of it is the work of the Holy Spirit. It comes to us with a guarantee. It is a sacramental, perhaps we may say, which keeps us united with Christ and with one another. We may find the "snippets" from the Bible, the "little chapters", often unsatisfactory, the antiphons often rather meaningless (especially when they are cut down, as they are on so many days of the year, to a word or two at the beginning of a psalm, and we have to wait for the end of it to say them in full). We may often find the versicles and responses (which—especially—call for a body of *singers*) simply tiresome. We shall come across a good many very bad hymns. We may be defeated by the elaborate system of commemorating incidental feasts (in which case we may omit them for our purpose without great loss). But we shall come to see that the Divine Office does indeed form, together with the Mass on which it depends, an annual cycle of which the lines are perfectly distinct. The liturgical seasons which we have briefly considered and the great feasts of the Universal Church will come to mean immeasurably more to us if we have some familiarity with the Office.

So far I have been laying a disproportionate emphasis on the difficulties. I must now try to bring out in rather more detail some of the advantages. When we begin to make the Psalter and the great Biblical canticles the substance of our daily prayer, we do realize at once that it is more than a prayer for the particular requirements of particular individuals (that is the sort of prayer which soon wears out, cannot be a staple diet for all our moods and tenses). And in saying that I am thinking not so much of the fact that the Psalter of the Office has been the spiritual food of Christians for so many centuries or of the way in which we unite ourselves in it with so vast a number of our contemporaries inside the cloister and out of it, but of its *style*, of the ways in which it throws open our communications with God. It is a very subtle style, yet easily intelligible. It does many things at once. It provides us with a continuous meditation on the history of Israel, that is, upon the beginnings of Christianity, a history which comes to acquire an increasing significance for us as we come to know more about Christianity and which at the same time *helps* us to know more about Christianity by that vital linking of the past with the future which was mentioned earlier. That is one reason why the "cursing psalms" occur in the Liturgy. They are part of the history of Israel. It is not a uniformly edifying history, but it is the history in which we find the working of God's providence. The history of Israel is so important because by its means the whole human race is to be drawn into union with the Three Divine Persons. And that leads to the second function which the style of the Office performs: it puts before our minds in the history of Israel all the great vicissitudes, spiritual and temporal, to which the human race is subject. It is the cry of the whole human race to God, in all its joys and sufferings, its triumphs and humiliations, its strength and weakness. And we both join in this cry, making it in some sort our own, and at the same time stand before God as intercessors for all who oppress and are oppressed, both for those who deface God's image and those who must struggle against them. There you have several more explanations of the "cursing psalms". What they amount to is that the psalms are *poetry*. The notion that the Church's prayer-book should not be poetry is, after a moment's thought, absurd. But it is not uncommon even in the minds of so-called educated people, which is a startling commentary on what is meant to-day by education.

Since, then, the style of the Office is a poetical style, it can contain a variety of meanings, and we are entitled to make use of any of them. We may meditate on the great psalm of the Law, the hundred and eighteenth (which is used for the day hours on Sunday, for instance), as a historical document, come to realize that it expresses the most sublime religious sentiments and make it gradually more and more our own prayer. Some psalms are prophetic of Christ in a very obvious way, for example the twenty-first, which he quoted on the Cross (if we look at it as a

whole the "cry of dereliction" will cease to be a problem for us).
As time goes on we shall find that the number of psalms which
we consciously treat as "messianic" has enormously increased.
And we shall begin to apply them also to Christ's second coming. For the whole of the Bible is prophecy in that sense, as
P. Daniélou has shown very finely in *Le Mystère de l'Avent*,[1] and
Christ himself is the prophet *par excellence*, the seer who sounds
the depths of Providence and who initiates its final phase before
the Last Day. As we begin to appreciate the meaning of inspira-
tion, of the Holy Spirit's activity in the history of God's people,
the mystical meaning of the Psalter will cease to seem unreal
and artificial. Even those passages which are textually corrupt
will be illuminated for us with a meaning of their own. We shall
find more and more in some verses of the Psalter the picture of
the Church, of the Church's Head in his full eschatalogical significance, of our Lady, the perfect Christian soul. A passage
from Mr Watkin's book will sum this up conveniently: "If ... a
formula of prayer thanks God for deliverance from some enemy
of our own day, its meaning is tied to that particular occasion. If
it thanks Him for deliverance from Sihon and Og, we are obviously expected to apply it to other enemies, whether the
spiritual enemies of our soul, or the human enemies of God and
His Church. Babylon, Jerusalem! What a host of interpretations
these leave open, not contradictory but complementary, as we
envisage various aspects of the city of the devil and the city of
God, interior or exterior, social or individual.[2]" (By this time the
difficulty about the "cursing psalms" should have been finally
removed.)

It is true that the Psalter will be very puzzling to those who
have little acquaintance with the history of Israel. But is it too
much to ask of the faithful—and in particular of the faithful
who belong to the professional classes—that they should have
at least as much acquaintance with it as the Psalter presupposes?
It is strange that people who would not readily confess to un-
familiarity with Shakespeare are sometimes content to know
next to nothing about the Old Testament. A knowledge of the
Psalter will lead naturally to the desire for a fuller knowledge of
the Old Testament, not to speak of the New. And thus that

[1] English ed. *Advent* (Sheed and Ward 1950).   [2] *Op. cit.* p. 9.

biblical culture, to which I have attributed so great an importance in the revival of the Liturgy, may perhaps become more
vigorous among us. The obvious way of acquiring this—the
way which the Church offers to us—is the reading of the Mattins
lessons, if not for every day of the year, at least for the Sundays
and the greater feasts. And that too is the obvious way of
acquiring the patristic culture, for the lessons of the Breviary
provide us also with a splendid introduction to patristic thought.
The selection and arrangement, it may be wise to repeat, will
probably not appeal to us in a good many cases. But the great
sermons of St Leo and St Augustine should make an immediate
appeal. Here we have what must be for the Christian some of the
greatest passages in the Latin language. And St Ambrose and
St Gregory, to take examples of writers who may prove less
attractive, will prove more and more informative on closer
acquaintance. It is, too, of great importance for an understanding of the Christian Mystery to contemplate it from the complementary point of view of the Greek Fathers; the Breviary will
supply us with the necessary materials.

It is hardly to be expected, though, I suppose, that many of
the laity should contrive to say the whole of Mattins. But Lauds
and Vespers for morning and night prayers (with Prime and
Compline, perhaps, as occasional alternatives) together with the
"little hours" of Terce, Sext and None, as opportunity serves, is
not an unreasonable programme for most people. The struc-
tures of Lauds and Vespers in the Roman Breviary are pretty
well the same. After the silent *Pater* and *Ave* and the versicle
which appeals for God's help, we have at Lauds three psalms,
an Old Testament canticle and a fourth psalm, at Vespers five
psalms. Then follows in each case a short Biblical text (the
"little chapter") a hymn and two versicles. Next comes the great
canticle of the hour, the Benedictus for Lauds, the Magnificat
at Vespers, with an antiphon before and after in each case. Some
intercessions follow on certain days; otherwise the collect is
then said, a few versicles and the antiphon of our Lady for the
season of the year with its own versicle and collect. Each hour
ends with the words: "May the divine assistance remain with us
always. Amen." The "little hours" consist in substance of a
hymn, three psalms, a little chapter, and a collect. It is not,

surely a very alarming programme. And if we follow it throughout the year (with some such help as Mr Sheppard's *Guide
to the Use of the Roman Breviary*)[1] we shall gain immense
profit.

No detailed commentary is possible on the texts of Lauds and
Vespers, even if we confined ourselves to the ordinary form for
a particular day of the week. What I would particularly recommend to you about Mr Watkin's book is that it supplies a
commentary, not only on the psalms as they occur throughout
the week but on many other elements of the Divine Office
throughout the year. His interpretations may not be altogether
acceptable to everybody, but he has demonstrated in a most
stimulating way the extent of the riches which lie waiting for
the Christian in the Divine Office. All I can do here is to suggest the lines of his treatment by a few references to his commentary on the Sunday psalms for Lauds and Vespers, which
occur so regularly also on feastdays. "The predominant theme
of Lauds", writes Mr Watkin, "is the Monarchy of God ... The
foundation of God's empire over His creatures is the fact that he
has created them and maintains them in existence. It is therefore
appropriate that the theme of the Psalms for Sunday ... should
be God the Creator-King. The Psalms chosen are xcii, xcix,
lxii, cxlvii. And the Canticle is the hymn of creation, the song of
the three children in Nebuchadnezzar's furnace. The selection is
of immemorial antiquity."[2] Mr Watkin goes on to point out
that until the revision of the Psalter psalms cxlix and cl were
added to psalm cxlviii, so that Lauds ended, as he puts it, "with
a prolonged peal of praise whose close is a Psalm of which every
verse is praise." (The Benedictine Breviary, amongst other
advantages, retains this arrangement.) A few headings only
must suffice from Mr Watkin's comments on these psalms.
"Psalm xcii displays the Creator-King triumphantly enthroned
above the floods and tempests of human life and history."
"Psalm xcix is a short psalm of praise to the Creator and moreover of His public worship." "Psalm lxii is individual. It is the
morning prayer of the awakening soul." "If the Psalms of Sunday Lauds are predominantly concerned with God, the Creator-
King, the Psalms of Sunday Vespers," Mr Watkin continues,

[1] London, 1927.   [2] *Op. cit.* pp. 34-5.

"may be profitably applied to His new Creation, the supernatural order of souls in grace, Christ's Mystical Body the
Church, the new and the highest Creation of the Creator-King."
So psalm cix, the first of these Sunday psalms, is the great
Messianic psalm *Dixit Dominus*, quoted by our Lord himself;
the next (cx) praises his wonderful works and his 'abiding
memorial' (which makes us think of the Eucharist); then we
have the picture of the "good citizen of God's kingdom" (cxi)
and the universal praise of the redeemed (cxii); in the last
psalm (cxiii) we have the great symbol of the Redemption, the
crossing of the Jordan.

Before I leave the subject of the psalms I must refer also to
Fr Foster's book *Psalms and Canticles of the Breviary*[1] and Dom
Ernest Graf's *The Church's Daily Prayer*,[2] which is a valuable
little book on the Divine Office in general.

The only texts in the Office on which it seems practicable to
comment here in any detail are those of the liturgical hymns.
These hymns are not known as they ought to be, I make bold to
say, even by Catholics who are professionally concerned with
literature. Partly, no doubt, the reason for this is the curious
prejudice against all Latin of post-classical periods. Another
reason, I am afraid, is that lack of theological culture of which
I have so often spoken, the dichotomy which exists in so many
people's minds, very often unconsciously, between Liturgy and
Literature, between religion and art. Perhaps what it comes
down to in the end is the dichotomy between intellect and will
which I shall discuss in the Epilogue. Even those who have an
appreciation of the Gregorian chant are sometimes blind to the
richness of the texts to which it is integrally bound. Let us take
first the hymn for midday, for Sext, which is attributed to St
Ambrose. I shall offer you an almost literal translation of it
with the English after each pair of Latin verses:

Rector potens verax Deus qui temperas rerum vices,
Powerful ruler and true God, you who govern the changes of
   things,
Splendore mane instruis et ignibus meridiem,
You who array the morning in splendour, the noon in fire,

---

[1] Mercier Press, 1947.   [2] Burns Oates and Washbourne, 1938.

Exstingue flammas litium, aufer calorem noxium,
Quench flames of strife, take from us heats of sin,
Confer salutem corporum veramque pacem cordium,
Give health of body and true peace of heart.

(The usual doxology follows.) That is not naïve, but straight-
forward and dignified, simple in the best sense of the word. It is
admirably condensed and the balance of the thought comes out
in the balance of the words. The language is not only pure but
distinguished. When we add to all this the perfect appropriateness of the theme to the period of the day which is now being
sanctified, we are entitled to say that this is in the absolute sense
a piece of great poetry. The impressive opening, *Rector potens*,
the felicity of the verbs *temperas* and *instruis*, and the curiously
effective persistence of "m" sounds are only a few of the points
which a full analysis would disclose. And there are the usual
characteristics of the liturgical style, the restraint which covers
a great depth of feeling, the tone of "high generality" and the
petition for both spiritual and corporal blessings.

It is not as though this were a particularly outstanding example of the liturgical hymn. There are many more equally good
and in some ways more striking. Twenty or thirty hymns are
attributed to St Ambrose alone, most of them with certainty,
the rest with various degrees of plausibility. Unfortunately—
and this is another and an important reason for the failure to
appreciate liturgical poetry at its proper worth—unfortunately
they were seriously mutilated by the Renaissance scholars who
carried out a general "revision" for the Breviary of 1632. Most
of the hymns were forced into classical language and classical
metres, and they have remained in that form in the Roman
Breviary ever since. The Benedictine (and in general the monastic) Breviary retains the original text; so does the Dominican.[1]
Here, for example, are the first three stanzas of the Vespers
hymn for Easter in the original form, the hymn of the
newly-baptized composed by an unknown author of the 7th
century:

---

[1] Cf. Byrnes, *Hymns of the Dominican Missal and Breviary,* B. Herder Book
Co. 1943, with Britt, *The Hymns of the Breviary Revised,* Burns Oates and
Washbourne, 1922.

Ad cenam Agni providi
Et stolis albis candidi,
Post transitum Maris rubri,
Christum canamus Principi

Cujus corpus sanctissimum
In ara crucis torridum
Cruore ejus roseo
Gustando vivimus Deo

Protecti Paschae vespere
A devastante Angelo,
Erepti de durissimo
Pharaonis imperio ...

And here are the same three verses "revised":

Ad regias Agni dapes,
Stolis amicti candidis,
Post transitum Maris rubri
Christo canamus Principi.

Divina cujus caritas
Sacrum propinat sanguinem
Almique membra corporis
Amor sacerdos immolat

Sparsum cruorem postibus
Vastator horret Angelus;
Fugitque divisum mare;
Merguntur hostes fluctibus.

It seems to me that you have only to listen to these two versions to realize that the first is a piece of accentual poetry, vigorous and fresh, the second a piece of quantitive verse, frigid, flat as a pancake and with all the savour drained out of it. Observe the alliteration, assonance and internal rhyme of the third (authentic) verse; sung as it should be sung to the traditional melody, it has an inevitable rightness. Try to sing the words of the other version instead!

Or compare the first verses in the two versions of the Mattins and Vespers Hymn for the feast of St Michael, ascribed to the 9th century writer Rabanus Maurus:

Tibi, Christe, splendor Patris,	*Te, splendor et virtus Patris,*
Vita, virtus cordium,	*Te, vita, Jesu, cordium,*
In conspectu Angelorum	*Ab ore qui pendent tuo,*
Votis, voce psallimus;	*Laudamus inter Angelos.*
Alternantes concrepando	
Melos damus vocibus.	

The first Vespers Magnificat antiphon for St Michael's is one of many antiphons in the Divine Office for which the Gregorian chant is not merely in good taste (the real Gregorian is always that) but exciting. At the dramatic words *Michael tuba cecinit* the notes fall steadily to produce a tension which is almost overpowering. *Canere* has always been the great Latin word for prophetic utterance, so what Michael did with his trumpet is hardly translatable—to say that he *sáng* on it is far too weak.

To conclude this subject (which is almost inexhaustible) I cannot resist referring to the great Sapphic hymn for the Feast of St John the Baptist which seems to have been written by Paul the Deacon in the 8th century. Its music is famous. Two small instances must suffice of its command over language. The first is taken from that part of the hymn used for first and second Vespers, the second is used at Mattins.

> *Ventris obstruso recubans cubili*
> *Senseras regem thalamo manentem*

Here St John is addressed: his first meeting with our Lord is described: "You, lying in the hidden cradle of the womb, had known the King still resting in his chamber" (*thalamo* is the bridal-chamber).

> *Cui latex haustum, sociata pastum*
> *Mella locustis*

"His drink was water and his food locusts and honey"—but "associated with locusts" is what the poet untranslatably says, and to prove that I have no anti-classical bias I refer you to

Horace's *Verba loquor socianda chordis*. But I prefer to be reminded (by *pastum*) of the hymn for Lauds of Christmas: *Parvoque lacte pastus est per quem nec ales esurit*. "With a little milk was he fed through whom not even the bird—*nec ales*—hungers".

A brief note must be added about the question of vernacular forms of the Office. The public performance of the Divine Office in the vernacular would not be attended by the same dangers as the introduction of a vernacular Mass, if only because it would not be a change at the very centre of things and would affect a smaller number of persons. In saying that I do not wish to be taken as recommending such a course except perhaps as a temporary expedient for religious communities in particular circumstances. The Office loses immensely in translation, although the nuns of Stanbrook have produced a most valuable English Breviary[1] which may be recommended for private use. The attempt to translate the Old Testament, in particular, into a "timeless" English which would be suitable for liturgical purposes, intelligible but not undignified, has proved of quite especial difficulty. Once more the conclusion imposes itself that we must restore a biblical mentality before we can hope to see our way at all clearly through all the obstacles which stand in the way of thoroughgoing liturgical revival. But this is clear: if the Divine Office is ever to become, as it once was, the food of mind and heart for the faithful at large, it cannot be our present Latin Office.

[1] *The Roman Breviary*, Burns Oates and Washbourne, 1937.

EPILOGUE

CHRISTIAN PERFECTION AND INTELLECTUALISM

PEOPLE WHO ASK ME TO ADDRESS THEM ARE OFTEN, I'M afraid, disappointed: they ask, it may be, for what is called in our jargon a spiritual conference, and find that they have let themselves in for a theological or (even worse, perhaps) a philosophical discourse; or they may have asked, taking their courage in both hands, for a philosophical or theological paper, only to find themselves, so far as they can see, listening to a sermon. The fact is that unless my nose is kept firmly to some particular grindstone, the subject to which I naturally gravitate is precisely the fusion, as I see it, of genuine metaphysics (which I use as a convenient term to embrace theology and philosophy) with genuine religion. That is what I mean by intellectualism.

It would be surprising if some of you at least didn't wish to interject at this point that I have no business to use the word in this sense. Intellectualism, you may wish to say, is commonly used only as a term of reproach. I know, and it is just that common usage which I want to resist. It seems to me misleading, and I shall try to show that it is based on a confusion. If this usage were completely established, it would be foolish to resist it, because meaning is determined by usage. But it is the business of those who consider that a word ought not to lose a good meaning to act, as Mr Fowler of *Modern English Usage* put it, as a "suspensory House of Lords" as long as they can. In the case with which I am concerned it is not merely a question of preserving a good meaning: what really matters is that, although the word intellectualism is in an advanced state of corruption, no other single word seems likely to indicate the point of view to which I have referred with any greater success, so that I am faced with the danger of not being able to refer to it compendiously at all.

It is obvious that there is a fallacy or a vice which is designated "intellectualism", and it would be unreasonable to complain that this should be so. Without for the moment going into the questions of just what is meant and ought to be meant by the intellect we can all agree that this fallacy or vice is always, whatever else it may prove to be, a lack of proper consideration for man's bodily functions. Whenever the word "intellectualism" is used as a reproach it is used with reference to some improper exclusiveness. It is the same with "rationalism" and "humanism". We use "rationalism" or "humanism" in a pejorative sense to refer to the exclusion from the scheme of things of anything higher than the human reason or the human person. But what happens when we want to indicate our own approval of rationality and the value of the human person? I suppose Maritain and Bremond between them have won acceptance for the expression "Christian Humanism", although it is still disliked in some quarters. If we can claim to be humanists in a proper sense, not in spite of being Christians but because of it, why are most of us so shy of calling ourselves in the same way intellectualists? We are not happy about using this word in reference to the spiritual part of us. There is plenty of excuse for not being happy about this; nevertheless I think it proves to be misleading if we reject this language, that is, more misleading than if we use it. That is what I shall try to show: that the word "intellectualism" ought not to be used only in contexts where it refers to a bad thing, but also in other contexts where it refers to a good thing. We must first consider in more detail what intellectualism in the bad sense—the only sense that can be called current among us at present—may be taken to mean.

The exclusiveness already noted indicates the general character of intellectualism in this sense. It may mean the excluding not only of bodily values, but also of moral, aesthetic or even religious ones. It may mean, then, a denial of proper importance to the imagination or the will. If Socrates really held that virtue is simply knowledge and vice is simply ignorance, then he is open to the charge of a false intellectualism, because he would be leaving out the factor of human freedom. Anyone who tried to reduce music to mathematics would be open to a similar charge because he would be leaving out an essential factor which we may refer to as "sensibility". At this point we might perhaps suppose that we need not discuss false intellectualism any further, that if we are to stake a claim for true intellectualism we have only to avoid various forms of exclusiveness in order to maintain the primacy of intellect. Intellect, then, is the supreme function of man which does not abolish or make nugatory but harmonizes and finalizes man's other powers. And this is, I would say, true. But there is still another sense in which intellectualism is used as a reproach, and this is the most important sense which has to be considered. For it directly challenges the primacy of the intellect. In this sense the function of the intellect is considered to be rational discourse: the discovery of universal essences or universal laws and the application of these discoveries to particular instances, the processes of the scientist and the historian, and the more abstract but similar processes of the logician and the philosophical systematizer. The reply is that all this overlooks what I believe to be the best usage of the word.

This usage is found, notoriously, in St Thomas, and the best way of introducing it into such a discussion as this is to recall what St Thomas has to say about the function of intellect in the Beatific Vision. His doctrine is that it is in virtue of the intellect that we are to be united with the object which beatifies us, with God seen face to face. There is a union between the knower and what is known: an intimate presence of what is known in the knower. St Thomas is contradicted by Scotus, according to whom beatitude consists essentially in an act not of intellect but of will; it is hard to believe that there can be any fundamental difference here, for Scotus, although his general line of thinking is decidedly different from St Thomas's, is surely talking about the same thing, about spiritual union, the supreme state of the soul in which it exercises that activity for which it was created, an activity which is at the same time a passivity, a possessing which is at the same time a complete submission. This is not to be described in terms of intellect alone as if we were excluding love. Rather we should agree, I think, that in so far as we can describe it at all, we find ourselves describing it as an apparent fusion of knowledge and love; that seems the best account we can give of real union: there is no separation between what we know and what we want, we are utterly satisfied in our knowing, there is nothing between us and our object. In the Post-Communion prayer in the Mass for peace we speak of God as him *quem nosse vivere, cui servire regnare est*—to know whom is to live, to serve whom is to reign. That sums it up.

St Thomas is surely right in emphasizing that we must speak of the intellect as the power in us by which this union is attained. It is our knowledge of the truth that gives us joy—*gaudium de veritate*. In the long run, then, everything turns on the fact that the soul is intellective, that it is, as St Thomas puts it, "capable of God". In the long run—but this brings us up against a serious difficulty: we may be satisfied that the final state of glory is to be described in intellectualist terms, but what about our present life? Are we to describe ourselves here and now as having an "intellectualist" programme? Here St Thomas does not give us so clear an answer. P. Rousselot in his great book *L'Intellectualisme de S. Thomas* suggests what I believe to be the answer which should follow from St Thomas's principles, as we have so far seen them: that is, that the end to which all our efforts should be directed is the contemplation of God (not for ourselves only, but, so far as in us lies, for others also). This may seem a commonplace. But a moment's thought will show us that it is not easy to combine it with other principles which are also considered commonplace. Don't we say that it is our love of God which matters, not our knowledge? Consider the following passage from Dom Stolz's book *The Doctrine of Spiritual Perfection*: "For the Fathers, *gnosis* (that is knowledge) bestowed assimilation to God, deification, whereas St Thomas resorts to or rather presupposes charity for that purpose, and that because he considers wisdom, like faith, as being in itself purely intellectual. The fact that, in this matter, St Thomas has recourse to charity reveals a conscious effort to guard against an excessively intellectual concept of Christian life"[1]. St Thomas, in fact, is unwilling to follow up his doctrine that grace is the seed of glory by assigning to us an intellectual union with God as our aim in this life. The union of charity is not for St Thomas a foretaste of the final end, Rousselot concludes; it is only the efficacious means to that end. So that when Rousselot claims

[1] p. 187 in Abbot Williams's translation.

that there is a practical identification, for St Thomas, of contemplation and the perfect life, we must question whether St Thomas would have accepted Rousselot's own view that mysticism is the supreme *intellective* activity which is the goal of all human life. That is the view—I believe it to be traditional —which I wish to put before you for your consideration in the altogether inadequate and summary way which is all that is possible for me in a lecture. What I propose to do is not so much to attempt any sort of demonstration of the thesis, but to throw some light on it, if I can, by freeing it from certain misapprehensions.

Even among ourselves there is a tendency to oppose "intellect" to "life". This is the most deadly of confusions. And at this point I ask leave to quote a page from the conclusion of my book *Certainty*[1] in which I comment on Rousselot's position: "Intellect is *life* in its highest form. Here is no factitious contrast between love and intellect, no shrinking from the 'realism' of mystical knowledge. Above all, the subject is seen in its broadest bearings, illuminating and co-ordinating every aspect of human activity. For a sane moral philosophy perfection lies in the full development of our nature; our nature is to know God and love him in this world as well as in the next. This is the *norm* which must direct our efforts. This is the end not only of our religious exercises, of all that complex system of rites and ordinances which seems so arbitrary to those outside it, but of each so-called trivial human action. Most of us must 'forsake Rachel for Lia' for most of our lives. We are obliged to devote our efforts in great measure to providing the merely material conditions of our own existence and that of others. But if we keep the true end in view we shall surely gain it, both for ourselves and others—for Christian perfection is no mere private indulgence in 'draughts of intellectual day'. It is only by making God our end, which means God's will—the salvation of all men—that we shall gain him. (Contemplation thus involves asceticism, that is, at bottom, the proper performance of our several duties, whatever it costs us). This may be done in a Carmelite's cell or by sweeping a crossing.

"If we do not think of theology to-day as 'the science of the

[1] Dacre Press, 1948.

saints', it is because we have ceased to think of it as one supreme science which bears on the whole of Christian living. Theology has tightened in one sense since St Augustine, but at the cost of parcelling out its riches. It has formed hard lumps which hang loosely together. What is called 'mystical theology' is no longer pervasive, and moral theology functions in a certain isolation from supernatural metaphysics. In speaking of Christian perfection, then, there is a danger of losing sight of our own first principles. When we say that what makes a man good is his willing effort, we must not be led into an unconscious anti-intellectualism. What makes a man good is (precisely) the gifts which God gives him; what makes him bad is his own rejection of them. We may say that man's goodness is in proportion to his acceptance, but it is the same to say that it is supremely important not to obstruct the effects of God's action upon us. This is the theme of the moralist, who naturally uses the language of co-operation rather than that of non-intervention. In the last analysis 'willing effort' refers to the exacting consequences of being God's instruments. Our part is to receive God's gift of himself. We are freed from sin only by grasping truth, by 'fixing' reality."[1]

That is, I am afraid, an overcondensed page from an over-condensed book, and I am grateful for the opportunity of expanding it. First I should like to take up the question of moral goodness. What do we mean when we say that sanctity, holiness, is not the same thing as knowledge? Certainly it is not the same thing as being learned in any particular field of knowledge. A man may be, from the academic point of view, abysmally ignorant, yet a saint. But can we talk about sanctity except in terms of knowledge of God? You may say, of course we can. A man may be a saint without knowing anything about theology. If by theology you mean the vocabulary and the systema-tizations of theological writers then the point is incontestable. But isn't there a traditional sense in which that old man in the church at Ars ("I look at God", you remember, "and he looks at me") was a theologian? And can we maintain the primacy of contemplation without admitting that it is the contemplation of God which makes us holy? This is the point at which, I expect, I shall encounter the strongest opposition, the critical point of the

[1] pp. 142-44.

paper, and it will be wise to admit at once that this last statement wears an air of paradox. The attempt to show that it is not
a paradox had better begin with a simple analysis of the most
ordinary moral situation. When we are faced with a moral
choice and we do the "right thing", what happens? We do what
we believe to be God's will for us at the moment. It may prove
that our action was misguided in the sense that we failed to perceive certain facts about the situation, but we did the "right
thing" all the same, that is, we had a right intention. And what
happened when we were making up our minds about it? We had
various motives pulling at us, and in the end we chose one of
them, deliberately allowed one of them to predominate by an
act of inattention to anything else. When we did the "right
thing", we said to ourselves "this is the reasonable course" or
"this is in conformity with the nature of things" or (it is all the
same) "this is God's plan"; moral obligation means the claim
upon us of God's plan. When we recognize the obligation we are
attending to God. It is the thought of God—though we may not
use these words about it—which makes us do the "right thing",
which attracts us away from the wrong thing. Conversely sin is
the shutting out of God from our minds. "Adam sinned",
St Augustine said, "when he fell from contemplation."

"An act of inattention to anything else" is a phrase used by
Abbot Chapman in one of his letters to describe the approach to
contemplative prayer. What I want to emphasize here is that we
are making this approach in some sort in every act which en-
gages our full personality, in every fully deliberate right act.
We may not describe to ourselves what we are doing in specifically religious language, but in so far as we deliberately choose to
do our duty we do so by refusing to be enticed by the more immediately attractive advantages of immoral conduct, and we
can only succeed in this refusal by concentrating upon the
absolute character of the moral claim, recognizing our obligation. We should admit without much hesitation that, although
we might describe ourselves as "not feeling at all religious" on
such occasions, we were in fact, to use the familiar language of
piety, "cleaving to God with our wills". What we should probably be less ready to allow is that we were therefore cleaving to
him with our intellects. Yet, when you come to think of it, it

must be so. We have slipped into a habit of considering the practice of religion and morality as an affair exclusively of the will. It doesn't make sense. When we say that good intention is the all-important thing, we must refer to a state of affairs in which our *minds* are bent upon God. It is really a knowledge of God. A habitually good intention is not just a static adherence to a set of rules drawn up by God. It is an increasingly sensitive awareness of the perfection to which each of us in his way is called by God. This means that we do come to know more of God himself. We should at least admit perhaps that we *want* more to know more of him. And if you think about this for a minute, just allow the significance of it to sink in, you realize that there must be a real though very obscure *contemplation* going on in us all the time when we are, as we should put it, trying to do our best. What I am referring to as "contemplative" or "intellectual" is thus something which is in itself the most ordinary thing in the world. It is in fact what *being a man* means if once you free it from the encrustations which so easily form over it. Working out syllogisms or sums, looking before and after, drawing inferences about the past and framing hypotheses about the future, *planning* of any kind (the business of "intellectuals" in the corrupt sense of the word)—all these things are useful and generally necessary as subsidiary functions of man. But that is all that they are. The essential business of man is experience, intuition—so submission to reality: that is what intellectualism ought to mean, and that is why it is a doctrine of love. As I see it, it is the great safeguard against misinterpreting charity, against giving it a sentimental or obscurantist sense, against setting it in any unreal opposition to truth. It underlines St John's magnificent phrase *do the truth*. It is the principle of genuine integration, of the proper hierarchizing of the human faculties. But before we pursue that subject there is more to be said about the meaning of moral goodness.

So far I have tried to make out that what we ordinarily mean by a good life is in the proper sense an intellectual affair, and that it flowers naturally—or should I say supernaturally?— into a more direct worship of God, a state of affairs in which a sharp distinction between religious practices and the daily business of life gives place to a certain merging of them. To draw attention to this I have had occasion to put it as follows: that Christianity is not a moralism but a mysticism. In other words our eternal reward is not something which is altogether extrinsic to our present duty. Union with God is what we have *now* to aim at, and we all know this; what we do not always recognize is that it has such humble beginnings, that it is the very framework of things in their normal condition. When St Paul tells us to pray always he isn't demanding the impossible. The worship of God is the end of man not as a remote eventuality but as an immanent life-giving principle. All this is only to say that the description of grace as the seed of glory isn't applicable only to the state of specially holy people, but is universally valid.

But the theme of "moral goodness" has still a couple of puzzles for us which at this juncture we can hardly avoid. In the passage quoted from *Certainty* what makes a man good was said to be the gifts which God gives him, and at the same time man's goodness was allowed to be in proportion to his acceptance of them. There are two factors involved, the giving and the receiving, and we can't help speaking of goodness in connection with each of them even when they don't go hand in hand. That is to say, a man who is offered grace in very large measure may not co operate with it by any means all along the line, yet he may still have great gifts, and I suppose (this is mere speculation) that he will reach the high place in heaven prepared for him after making up for lost ground in Purgatory (or, according to another view, just a lower place in heaven than he was intended to reach). In contrast with him, mustn't we be prepared to allow that there might be men who weren't called to the same heights but yet corresponded more exactly with the graces offered to them? We could hardly avoid calling them better in a sense than the first man, although they might never reach his eventual eminence. (I repeat that this is mere speculation, but it might have seemed like shirking a question to say nothing about it.) The difficulty about answering that it is simply our co-operation with grace that assigns to us our degree of glory, and that this is what ought to be meant by goodness, is that if you leave out of account any antecedent arrangement on God's part you seem to reduce predestination to mere foreknowledge.

In any case it is in view of the gifts which it enables us to receive that our co-operation is called our goodness. It is union with God, the knowledge and love of him, which makes us what we are meant to be. And that is surely the fundamental meaning of goodness: perfection or completion.

So much for the first of the two puzzles about moral goodness. We have now the clue to the second, which bears on the goodness which we attribute to certain activities whether or not they spring from a good intention. How are we to connect with one another these two sorts of moral goodness? A man is good, we may say, in so far as his actions tend to his completeness, to the purpose for which he has been created. Even when his action had a bad motive, it may still be good in the sense that it helps to bring about those conditions in which the end of man may be more effectively pursued by others, and, if he is prepared to use them, by the agent himself. As St Thomas puts it, giving alms is a good thing (*normally*, perhaps one should add) even when the motive is vain glory. This sort of goodness I propose to call material goodness as opposed to formal goodness or goodness of intention. The point which I want to emphasize here is that action cannot be called properly good even in the formal sense unless the agent *thinks* that it is also materially good. We must be on our guard against Kant's anti-intellectualist view of good intention which evacuates it of content. To do our duty is to aim at least at contributing to the development of God's plan, to hold before our minds the purpose to which our actions must somehow or other contribute, that is, the union of all creatures with their Creator. We may say that formal goodness is the beginning and end of morality: good intention *is* prayer, worship, union, and it develops itself or rather allows God to develop it towards its consummation; but it develops through material goodness. It is true that, if for accidental reasons a man's spiritual development is retarded in this life, if the conditions for his development are not present owing to the malice or stupidity of others, or (it may be) owing simply to his own stupidity, it will receive development in the next (a man may remain through no fault of his own ignorant of the true nature of material goodness). Whether the development received in the next life stands in a relation of proportion to the development received in this life is a question which I must leave aside. But it is clear that, in the sort of case which we have been considering, we must speak of a lack of goodness here and now as a result of this sort of stupidity. It is, too, an extreme case. In practice a man of genuinely good intention is keenly aware of the relative values of human activities, of the need for arranging them in an intelligible hierarchy and of co-ordinating them towards the final end; he does not in fact confuse means with ends. The saints, *qua* saints, have a better practical judgment than the rest of us. They may not use intellectualist language about it, but they are intellectualists. When they call the will our highest faculty they must not be taken as attacking the fundamental principles of Thomist psychology.

It may still be suggested that I am overlooking non-intellectual values—the values, say, to which we refer when we speak of a man's character or of affective or aesthetic values, so I shall say a few words about each of them. The *Times Literary Supplement* published a number of articles and letters in March 1949 on the subject of intellect, and some particularly pertinent remarks were made about character. When we oppose character to intellect, it was pointed out, we are really emphasizing the importance of physiological characteristics and showing the limits within which our free rational activity operates. But it is free rational activity which is in the last analysis what matters. The discussions to which I refer were hampered by a failure to recognize the intuitive or contemplative character of intellect; they therefore missed the essential point and the profound implications which flow from it; but they were a sign of a healthier tone in public debate of this kind, despite a good deal of nonsense from correspondents who professed to believe themselves incapable of freedom in the sense of responsible choice.

The point just made about character bears also on the subject of affective values. Human affection at its highest—the real thing—rises above the biological level and above purely self-regarding motives of any kind, and attaches itself to the objective qualities of the beloved. What we are considering here is our power to value persons and things for their own sakes, to make way for them and appreciate them. What we do for them externally is a sign of our appreciation and in the interests of the objective qualities. What else can we call this power to appreciate but intellect? It may become clearer that it is power of acceptance, of submission and loyalty to reality. I hope this will remind you of Gabriel Marcel, and I believe he would agree with me in saying that all forms of genuine charity are forms of fidelity or truthfulness.

"Still", you may say, "intellect is not the whole man; there is the claim of 'feeling'. Are you denying any ultimate value to the artist's activity?" No, indeed I am not. The artist's activity I would call eminently intellective. It is impossible to present the case for this conclusion in a satisfying way without a detailed analysis, but it may be a sufficient pointer to suggest the view that sensation itself—human sensation that is (let us keep the brutes out of it)— is intellectual. I can claim the support of other Catholic philosophers for rejecting the clear-cut distinction between intellection and sensation which you will find in the Thomist manuals. To put the point as briefly as possible, we have not two distinct powers of awareness, but only one. If there is such a thing as a pure sensation without an intellectual awareness, it is outside our experience: our faculty of awareness bears in the first place on our bodies and other bodies in contact with them—and as such we call it sensation—and upon this basis it makes further analyses and distinctions within the real and rises to the knowledge of the super-sensible, of God—and as such we call it intellection, but sensation is not something outside intellection, in this view, but its first stage. Thus we can speak of an intellective intuition of the particular material thing in so far as we come in contact with it, and we have our answers to those who would make of intellect simply an *abstractive* faculty. The mere awareness of muscular pressure is intellective. The artist's activity is eminently intellective because he works with the materials gained by the intellect on the sense-level and perceives in them patterns, relationships, analogies and associations. He lives more intimately with reality than the special scientist, for his concern is not just with what things have in common, their universal aspects and the laws which govern them, but with the relationship of concrete particulars seen in their totality, with the richly unified pattern, say, which all these sounds taken together and undiluted, as it were, form in the perceiving mind avid for the richness and unity of God.

"Feeling", then, as it is used in the language of literary and artistic criticism, so far from referring to something opposed to intellect, refers, if I am right, precisely to the keenness of intellect. Generalizing this result, we may say that the various emotions register the free play of intellect or the hampering of it. Intellect will not be its true self unless it generates or develops into an emotion. We have only to consider what we mean when we say that we are really *interested* in somebody or something. Thus there is no question, on this showing, of trying to discover an "act of the whole man" which somehow transcends the intellect. The attempt to canonize a form of activity which sets in motion all the various functions of man at the same time is illusory and dangerous. It is illusion, because we cannot in fact combine all our various functions in an equal degree of intensity: you cannot do gymnastic exercises and properly appreciate a symphony at the same time. It is dangerous, because it denies the hierarchical structure of man's being. It denies the subordination of the bodily powers to the spiritual. The truth which it is distorting is that the soul needs the body, not to combine with it by some sort of fusion into a mysterious higher synthesis, but for its own proper development. The human soul cannot begin to exercise its activity without the body, which is its means of contact with outside reality, but the relation of body to soul is always that of servant to master.

It is that very simple and obvious truth which is safeguarded, I believe, by the intellectualist position which I have tried to outline. Apart from this, all that it seeks to do is to remind us of what we must mean by the soul, that its essential activity is immanent yet in the exact sense of the word ecstatic, or, in St Augustine's simpler and profounder words that "we are not our own". A paper with the title "Christian Perfection and Intellectualism" would be commonly supposed, I suspect, to be a disquisition on the importance of scholarship. Here, on the other hand, I am concerned to suggest that in a sense scholarship is overrated amongst Catholics. I don't mean that we have a surplus of fine scholars; obviously we could do with many more. But in a decadent age it is easy for us to be infected with the idolatry of scholarship which acts as a substitute for the true culture of the mind. We know that the cure for this and for all disorders is, in a word, the Liturgy, the source of contemplation; that is, the only possible solution to important problems, whether national, international or personal, lies in the *practical* adoption (we all pay lip-service to it) of St Benedict's maxim that nothing is to be preferred to the work of God. The Liturgy is the supreme apostolate; it is the Church herself, whose life is the Liturgy, who is the supreme witness to the Resurrection. The considerations which I have put before you are quite without value unless they help to illustrate this truth. Christian Intellectualism, as I see it, is nothing if not liturgical.

INDEX OF AUTHORS' NAMES

(other than Biblical)